ABOUT THE BOOK

Basketball is booming, not only as a professional sport but in high schools and colleges as well. The rule changes of the eighties have made the game even faster and more exciting. This book provides an up-to-the-minute account of basketball, its history, rules and methods of scoring. It describes shots, tactics, skills and equipment, explains basketball terms, and includes profiles of some of the leading players both past and present.

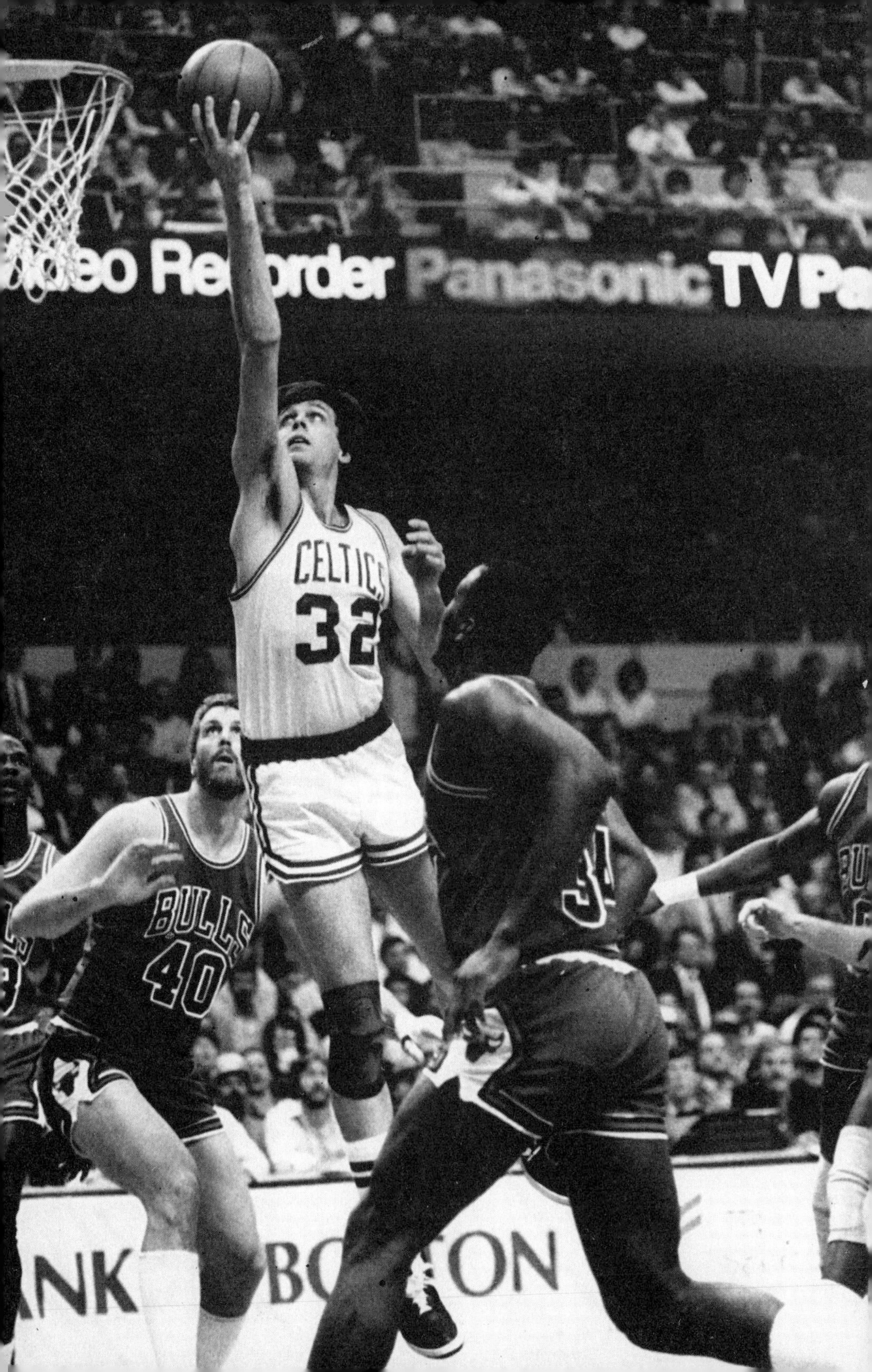
Recorder Panasonic TV
32
BULLS
40

ALL ABOUT
BASKETBALL

George Sullivan

Illustrated with photographs and diagrams

G. P. PUTNAM'S SONS • *New York*

G. P. Putnam's Sons, a division of Penguin Putnam Books for Young Readers,
345 Hudson Street, New York, NY 10014.
Published simultaneously in Canada.
Printed in the United States of America.
Book Design by Joy Taylor

Library of Congress Cataloging-in-Publication Data

Sullivan, George
All about basketball / George Sullivan.
p.   cm.
Includes index.
Summary: Gives an overview of the history and the rules of the game of basketball, along with
discussion of various plays and profiles of famous players.
1. Basketball—Juvenile literature. 2. Basketball—United States—History—Juvenile
literature. [1. Basketball.] I. Title.
GV885.S85 1991
796.323—dc20   91-10141   CIP   AC

ISBN 0-399-61268-8 (hardcover)

10 9

ISBN 0-399-21793-2 (paperback)

10

*Frontispiece: In recent seasons, pro basketball has shown excit-
ing growth. Here, the Boston Celtics' Kevin McHale glides in for
two points in a game against the Chicago Bulls.*

Many people helped in the preparation of this book by providing background information and photographs. Special thanks are due to Jerry Healy and Wayne Patterson, Basketball Hall of Fame; Lou Kern and Joe Favorito, Fordham University; Larry Baumann, New York University; Dave Saba, University of Texas; Francesca Kurti, TLC Photos; Barbara and John Devaney; Patrick Calkins, Aime LaMontagne, and Tim Sullivan.

CONTENTS

1

BUSTIN' LOOSE

They wear sneakers provided free by shoe companies. They appear on television and travel to national tournaments. Some are nationally known. Their teams get spotlighted each week in the "Super 25" rankings in *USA Today*.

We're not talking about professional basketball players or even college stars. The pros and colleges have their own sets of rewards.

No, all of the benefits mentioned above apply to high school basketball players, to fifteen- and sixteen-year-old schoolboys. (School*girls* don't qualify; not yet, anyway.)

Basketball, a fast and colorful sport that's been around for a little bit more than a century, is enjoying a period of exciting growth. And what's been happening in high school basketball is only one sign of the times.

Basketball is booming as a college and professional

sport, too. Many millions of fans crowd gyms and arenas to watch their favorite teams. Millions more tune in on television.

It's not hard to understand basketball's appeal. It's a sport of feeling, of emotion. As a spectator, you're close enough to the players and coaches to see their reactions. You can hear the squeak of sneakers on the hardwood floor. You get involved when you watch basketball.

For the most part, basketball games are played in cozy arenas, not huge stadiums as in football and baseball, where the players can look like ants to spectators. In basketball, fans are close up. Their noise can raise the roof. In college games in the Big Ten Conference, teams sometimes have to move off the bench and go out onto the court during timeouts. Otherwise, the players and coaches wouldn't be able to hear each other.

Basketball Takes Off

Basketball began to zoom in popularity during the 1970s. In part at least, this popularity resulted from the frequent televising of college games. Today, the National Collegiate Athletic Association's men's

Basketball is a sport of feeling, of emotion. Here Kevin Johnson of the Suns rejoices after a Phoenix basket.

Some 550 colleges and 16,500 high schools have women's teams. Above, Purdue faces New Mexico State.

championship tournament, held each March, ranks with the World Series and Super Bowl as the nation's major sports events.

On the high school level, basketball has long been the No. 1 sport. More basketball is played than any other sport. Approximately 17,000 high schools sponsor boys' teams, and some 16,500 high schools have girls' teams.

It used to be that high school basketball stars were

known only to their classmates or perhaps citywide. Now top teams representing the National Federation of State High School Associations get national exposure. For example, many are featured in the game-of-the-week presentations broadcast by SportsChannel America.

Outstanding players from teams such as Martin Luther High School in Chicago, *USA Today's* No. 1 team in 1990, became nationally known. Of course, they get their Nikes (or some other sneakers) free.

In days past, high school teams rarely crossed state lines to compete. But nowadays there are scores of national tournaments offering competition, more than thirty of them in December alone. They range from the wintertime Beach Ball Classic in Myrtle Beach, South Carolina, to the Holiday Prep Event held in December in Las Vegas. Schools that are nationally ranked get expense-paid trips to such events.

Changing the Game

What's been happening in high school basketball in recent years is a spillover from the tremendous interest in college basketball, which went through a period of revolutionary change during the 1980s.

For years, delaying tactics had tainted the college game. A team with a big lead wouldn't even try to score, but would simply hold the ball, "freeze" it, until time ran out. College basketball was often referred to as "stall ball."

The rule makers changed that. In 1985–86, a 45-second clock was introduced. A college team had to shoot within 45 seconds or lose possession of the ball. (Women's college basketball already had a 30-second shot clock.)

Another important change had to do with scoring. In high schools and colleges field goals had always been worth 2 points, while a free throw counted as 1 point. Beginning in 1985–86, college basketball introduced the 3-pointer. Any field goal taken from beyond a line 19 feet, 9 inches from the basket counts as 3 points. All other field goals still count as 2 points.

The new rules have changed stall ball to speed ball. Run 'n' gun has become the order of the day. Teams push the ball up the court fast, fire long passes, and then take quick shots off the break. On defense, teams press and gamble for steals. The idea is to get possession as quickly as possible and start attacking again on offense.

Scores have gone through the roof. Early in January 1991, Los Angeles' Loyola Marymount beat U. S. International, 186–140, to establish the NCAA scoring record. It lasted about a month. In mid-February that year, it was broken when Troy State, a little known Alabama school, topped DeVry Institute, 187–117.

The fans love it. Everywhere, attendance has boomed.

The Pro Game

As for professional basketball, it has had a 3-point rule since 1979 and a 24-second clock since 1954.

In 1989–90, the National Basketball Association (NBA), basketball's top professional league, enjoyed its seventh consecutive season of growth. The League drew more than 17 million fans that season, averaging more than 15,000 per game.

Another measure of the growth of the pro game is the spiraling value of teams. There was a time when some owners couldn't give away their franchises, their right to operate as part of the NBA. Nobody wanted them.

Compare that to what happened in 1988 and 1989, when the Miami Heat, Charlotte Hornets, Minnesota Timberwolves, and Orlando Magic became members of the NBA. Each paid $32.5 million just for the privilege of joining the NBA.

Pro players such as Michael Jordan, Magic Johnson, Patrick Ewing, Larry Bird, and David Manning have all helped to boost basketball's popularity. Each of these players has enormous appeal. Their moves and shots are copied on playgrounds and school gyms all over America.

NBA basketball is also booming overseas. Zambia, Finland, and more than seventy other foreign countries now broadcast NBA games on television. It is estimated that basketball is now played in some 130 countries worldwide. A tournament each fall pits an NBA team against the best foreign teams.

Pro basketball has no immediate plans to put franchises in foreign cities, but it's certainly a possibility for the future. The Phoenix Suns and Utah Jazz played the first game of their 1990–91 schedule in Japan. In London, kids wear Los Angeles Lakers T-shirts, and jackets with NBA logos are popular in Paris. Basketball has become a truly international sport.

Pro stars such as the Bulls' Michael Jordan have helped to boost basketball's popularity.

2

A LOOK BACK

Unlike other sports, whose beginnings are a bit uncertain, basketball has a birthday. The date of the first basketball game is known with absolute accuracy.

That's because basketball was invented. It did not evolve from other sports. Football, for instance, sprang from soccer and rugby. Baseball is a close relative of the English game of rounders.

The man who thought up basketball was a Canadian, Dr. James Naismith. The time was 1891. The place was Springfield, Massachusetts.

Naismith was thirty years old at the time. He had been born in Almonte, Ontario, and had attended McGill University in Montreal. After studying for the ministry for three years, Naismith decided his real interest was in physical education. He enrolled in the International Young Men's Christian Association Training School in Springfield, Massachusetts. (Today, the school is known as Springfield College.) Be-

Dr. James Naismith, basketball's inventor.

fore long, Naismith joined the faculty as an instructor in physical education.

During the cold Massachusetts winters, Naismith's gym class was forced to remain indoors. Students quickly became bored with their usual regimen of calisthenics.

Naismith decided to offer games instead. His first idea was to adapt some popular outdoor game for indoor play. He tried football, but found that it was too rough a game to play on a hard gym floor. Soccer proved impractical, too, as many players ended up bruised from falls.

"Basket Ball"

Naismith made up his mind to invent a new game, one that was easy to learn and could be played by many students. He decided the game should have a ball, and that it should be a large ball. This was because a sport that employed a small ball, such as a baseball or a tennis ball, would also require an instrument with which to hit it. That feature could make the sport difficult to learn. Naismith decided to use a soccer ball for his new game.

Naismith realized that he could not permit players to run with the ball, which involved too much physical contact. To advance the ball, players would have to pass it.

In addition, the game had to have a goal, Naismith decided. So he had boxlike goals put at each end of the court. Then he realized that the players on the defensive team could prevent scoring simply by clustering in front of the goal and blocking the ball with their bodies.

The solution was to elevate the goal. This forced

players to shoot the ball on an arc, making accuracy more important than brute strength.

Naismith asked the building custodian for a pair of boxes, each 18 inches square. The custodian told Naismith he didn't have suitable boxes but that he'd give him a pair of peach baskets.

In Naismith's gymnasium, an elevated running track circled the floor like a balcony. Naismith instructed the custodian to nail a peach basket to the lower rim of the track at each end of the floor. It happened that each basket rim was placed 10 feet above the floor. That's the regulation height of baskets today.

One day in mid-December 1891, Naismith divided his gym class of eighteen men into two nine-man teams. "Throw the ball into the basket," he told them.

The playing area was small, only 35 feet by 50 feet. (A regulation basketball court today is 50 feet by 94 feet.) The players wore long, tight-fitting gym pants and long-sleeved jerseys. There was little teamwork. As soon as one player got hold of the ball, all of the others closed in on him. Shouts of "Pass it! Pass it!" echoed through the gym. Only one goal was scored during that first experiment with the game.

Naismith now had a game to entertain his gym class, but the game had no name. One of Naismith's students suggested calling it "Naismith ball." Naismith vetoed that suggestion, opting instead for the name "basket ball." The name stuck, but it wasn't until the 1920s that this term began to be used regularly as one word.

During January 1892, the first regulation basketball game was played. There were seven men to a side. In later years, this would be changed to nine players, then to eight, and finally to five.

Women were involved with the sport right from the

beginning. Teachers from Buckingham Junior High School in Springfield formed the first women's team in 1891. Vassar and Smith, both women's colleges, added basketball to their activity schedules during the fall of 1892.

As the game grew in popularity, sporting-goods manufacturers began turning out special "basket balls," which were slightly larger than a soccer ball. Peach baskets were replaced by net baskets attached to a metal rim. When a goal was scored, the game

Basketball at Smith College in Northampton, Massachusetts, in 1906, the class of 1908 vs. the class of 1909.

was halted so that someone could fish the ball out of the net. In 1905, the open-bottomed net was introduced, permitting the ball to drop straight through to the floor. About the same time, backboards were used for the first time.

Revising the Rules

During the late 1800s and early 1900s, Naismith made rule changes from time to time. For instance, advancing the ball only by passing it didn't provide enough action, and running made for too rough a game. The compromise Naismith settled upon was to advance the ball by bouncing it—by dribbling it, that is.

For several years, players were permitted to dribble with both hands. But the two-handed dribble was done away with in 1898.

Two other revisions in the rules came about because of a problem that had developed. Naismith had hung the peach baskets 10 feet from the floor. Average-size people of the 1890s stood 5-foot-6 or 5-foot-7. The peach baskets were beyond their reach, and the ball had to be arched high into the air to land in the basket.

The problem was that a player who was taller than average could easily dominate a game. When shooting the ball this player was closer to the basket,

BASKET BALL
OUTFITS.

INDOOR BASKET.

The baskets are strong iron hoops, with braided cord netting, arranged to be secured to a gymnasium gallery or wall for indoor use, or on an upright pipe the bottom of which is spiked to be driven into the ground for outdoor use. By means of a cord the ball is easily discharged after a goal is made.

Indoor Goals, per pair,	$15.00
Outdoor Goals, per pair,	30.00
No 10 Association Foot Ball, each,	3.25
American Rubber Foot Ball,	1.25

Prices for Special Portable Baskets for Exhibitions in Halls or low priced outfits given on application

The basket as it was pictured in an 1893 rulebook.

which made it easier for him to score. His height also gave him an advantage on rebounds. He could snatch the ball over the heads of the smaller players as it caromed off the backboard or rim.

The taller-than-average player also prevailed whenever there was a center jump. And, as Naismith had planned the game, there was an abundance of center jumps. Each period began when the referee tossed the ball up between two players at midcourt, who would jump and try to tap the ball to a teammate. There was also a center jump after each basket, after each successful free throw, and whenever a held ball was called—that is, when two opposing players got possession of the ball at the same time.

A team with a tall player would assign him to participate in the center jump. Since the tall player was able to control virtually every tap, his team had possession of the ball through much of the game.

To make the game more fair, the amateur sports officials who served as basketball's rule makers decided to do away with the center jump, except at the start of a period or in the event of a held ball. After a field goal or a successful free throw, the ball was given over to the team that had not scored.

A rule adopted in the 1930s established a zone under the basket. No offensive player was permitted to stay longer than three seconds within this zone. The rule prevented a tall man from "basket-hanging," planting himself close to the basket and remaining there until a teammate got the ball to him or a rebound came within reach.

The 3-second rule and the rule that eliminated a center jump after every basket helped to bring the game into balance. No longer did a tall man necessarily make a team superior.

The 10-second rule was adopted in 1932. This rule

states that the offensive team must advance the ball across the halfcourt line within 10 seconds of getting possession or lose the ball to the opposition.

These changes in the rules did a great deal to speed up play. It wasn't long before basketball became the running game it is today.

Growth of the Sport

Everywhere Naismith's students went, they introduced the new game. A short time after its invention, basketball was being played in YMCA gyms throughout the United States and Canada.

Colleges also took up the game. The first contest between two colleges took place on February 9, 1895, when the Minnesota State School of Agriculture crushed Hamline University of St. Paul, 9–3.

The first eastern collegiate game matched two Pennsylvania schools, Haverford and Temple. The date was March 23, 1895. Haverford won, 6–4.

The college game grew by leaps and bounds. By 1905, more than forty colleges had basketball teams.

The 1930s brought many changes. Frank Keaney, coach of Rhode Island State College, introduced an era of high-scoring, freewheeling basketball. His team was one of the first to use the fast break, and the team did plenty of shooting.

In 1937, Stanford's Hank Luisetti pioneered a one-

hand style of shooting in leading his team, the Indi-
ans, to the Pacific Coast Conference title. Luisetti
scored 1,596 points during his college career, an all-
time college record.

The same year, 1937, the first big national postseason tournament, the National Invitational Tournament (NIT), made its debut in Madison Square
Garden in New York City. Six teams competed. Temple University of Philadelphia defeated New York's
Columbia University, 60–36, to win the first NIT
championship.

What is today college basketball's most glittering
college tournament, the NCAA (National Collegiate
Athletic Association) tournament, got started in 1938.
In the final, the University of Oregon met Ohio State
at Patten Gymnasium on the campus of Northwestern
University in Evanston, Illinois. Oregon won, 46–43.
The NCAA held its first tournament for women in
1982.

Professional basketball was tried as early as 1898,
with the National Basketball League. The league
folded in 1903.

During the 1920s, a professional team named the
New York Celtics, often called the "Original Celtics,"
won widespread fame. In 1921–22, the Celtics won
the championship of the Eastern League. They then
toured the country, traveling from city to city to play

the best teams. During their tour, the Celtics won 194 of 204 games.

In 1926, the Celtics joined the American Basketball League, which had gotten off the ground the year before. They won the league title two years in a row. Bored fans stopped going to the games because they were sure the Celtics were going to win. In professional competition, the team amassed an incredible 1,320 wins against only 66 losses.

The National Basketball Association (NBA), today the world's foremost professional league, had its beginnings in 1946. It operated as the Basketball Association of America (BAA) until 1949, when it changed its name to the one it uses today.

Flip through the pages of the *NBA Guide*, published each year by *The Sporting News*, and glance at the pictures of the early NBA championship teams. Every player is white. That's because basketball, like baseball and other major sports, did not allow black players to participate.

When Chuck Cooper, a 6-foot-6 All-America selection from Duquesne University, signed with the Boston Celtics in 1950, he became the first black player in the NBA. By the 1960s, black players had come to dominate pro basketball.

College basketball was largely all white until about 1950, when the racial barriers started coming down.

By the mid-1960s, all major college teams had black players.

James Naismith died in 1939, but he lived long enough to see basketball become a major sport, not only in the United States but in foreign countries as well. By 1940, basketball's rules were being printed in thirty languages.

Basketball became an Olympic sport in 1936. Naismith, then seventy-five, attended the ceremonies in Berlin honoring basketball. Twenty-two nations entered teams. The United States won the gold medal, and would not lose a game in Olympic basketball competition until 1972. Women's basketball became an Olympic sport in 1976.

By that time, basketball had become the world's most popular indoor sport. Not bad for a game that began with a soccer ball and a couple of peach baskets.

3

SOME BASICS

From the days of James Naismith, every basketball game has started with a center jump. Two opposing players, usually the teams' centers, face each other at the court's center circle. An official tosses the ball into the air above the two players, who leap up and try to tap it to a teammate. The clock starts as soon as a tap is picked up by another player.

Playing Time

The playing time of a game varies, depending on the level of competition. A high school game lasts 32 minutes, and is divided into two 16-minute halves (four 8-minute quarters). The teams take a 1-minute break at the end of the first and third quarters, and a 10-minute break between halves.

College teams play a 40-minute game, divided into

two 20-minute halves. There's a 15-minute break at halftime.

In the NBA, a game is 48 minutes in length. It is divided into four 12-minute quarters. There's a 1½-minute break after the first and third quarters and a 15-minute break between halves.

Although the playing time of a professional game is 48 minutes, it usually takes more than two hours for the game to be played. During the 1989–90 season, games averaged 2 hours, 7 minutes. That's because play is stopped whenever an official calls a foul, the ball goes out of bounds, or a team calls a timeout.

Many teams save their timeouts for the desperate final minutes of a game, when coaches like to plot strategy with players. A pro team is allowed seven timeouts, each 100 seconds in length, plus a 20-second timeout in each half. Play is also stopped at the end of each quarter. In addition, there are two timeouts for television commercials.

The final period of a championship playoff game between the Detroit Pistons and Portland Trail Blazers in 1989–90—12 minutes of playing time—consumed 55 minutes, 57 seconds. It was part of a 2-hour, 43-minute game won by the Pistons. The final 3 minutes of playing time took 31 minutes. The final 31.5 seconds required 11 minutes, 17 seconds.

In professional play, as well as in college and high school, if the score is tied at the end of regulation time, teams play as many overtime periods as are needed to determine a winner. In professional and college ball, an overtime period lasts 5 minutes. High school teams play 3-minute overtimes.

The Shot Clock

For a game of basketball, you need a ball, a backboard, and a level place to play. If you want to be sure the game is going to be exciting, you need one other piece of equipment—a shot clock. In pro basketball, a team must shoot within 24 seconds of gaining possession of the ball. The clock that keeps track of the seconds is a digital display above the backboard. Everyone watching or playing keeps an eye on the clock. "It's the heartbeat of the game," says one *Sports Illustrated* article.

The shot clock in pro basketball was first used in the 1954–55 season. In the years before the shot clock was instituted, the pro game struggled. A team's offensive strategy usually consisted in getting a lead and then stalling, passing endlessly, seldom making any attempt to score. The defending team's strategy was usually to commit a foul as soon as possible, then attempt to get possession of the ball following the free throw.

A low point was reached in a game on November 22, 1950, when the Fort Wayne Pistons defeated the

In college basketball, the shot clock sometimes looks like this.

Minneapolis Lakers by a score of 19–18. The Pistons won by simply holding on to the ball, passing and dribbling, taking only "can't miss" shots. The score at the end of the first period was 8–7. The spectators felt as if they had been cheated.

Several rule changes had been tried to solve the

problem of stalling, but none had worked. Then Danny Biasone, owner of the NBA's Syracuse Nationals, came up with a unique solution: the shot clock. Till then, teams had been taking about 60 shots a game combined, Biasone observed. His objective was to raise the average number of shots per game to 120.

A game was 48 minutes long, or 2,880 seconds. Biasone divided 120 shots into 2,880. The answer: 24. Biasone set the shot clock at 24 seconds.

Biasone got other NBA owners to come to Syracuse to watch a demonstration game in which each team had to shoot at the basket within 24 seconds of getting possession. The rule transformed the game. Players realized that not making an effort to get off a good shot resulted in taking a bad one as the shot clock wound down—or losing possession. Stalling simply wasn't possible.

Defensive teams quickly saw that deliberate fouling was no longer necessary when trying to get possession. All you had to do was wait. Within 24 seconds, you'd have a chance for a rebound, or you'd get the ball following a basket.

The owners liked what they saw. The shot clock was tried in preseason games that fall. It worked so well that it was adopted for the 1954–55 season.

The shot clock immediately speeded up games and boosted scoring. In 1947–48, the highest-scoring team in the league, the Chicago Stags, had averaged

75.8 points per game. In 1954–55, the first season with the clock, NBA teams averaged 92.6 points. In 1981–82, the Denver Nuggets established the highest team scoring average ever—126.5 points.

Today, only high school basketball is played without a clock. In college basketball, the men's game is played with a 45-second clock and the women's with a 30-second clock.

The professional game's rule makers have never tampered with the 24-second rule. The shot clock is as much a part of the pro game today as 7-foot players, whopping salaries, and entertainment by jugglers and expert dribblers at halftime.

The Court

A regulation basketball court is 94 feet long and 50 feet wide. For high school play, however, the court may be 84 feet in length.

The free-throw line, from which foul shots are taken, is 15 feet from the backboard.

The free-throw line is at the center of a circle that is 12 feet in diameter. When a jump ball is called in that half of the court, it takes place within this circle. Only the two players jumping are allowed within it.

From the foul line to the end line, there are two parallel lines 12 feet apart (16 feet in the professional game). These form the free-throw lane, which has

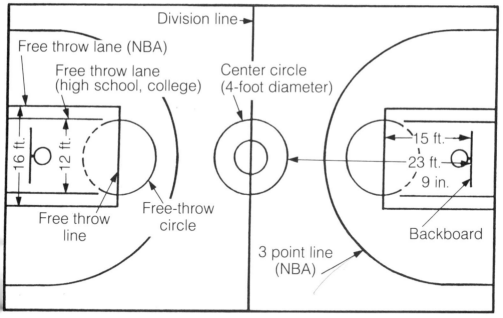

Free throw lane (NBA)

Free throw lane
(high school, college)

Division line

Center circle
(4-foot diameter)

16 ft.

12 ft.

Free throw
line

Free-throw
circle

3 point line
(NBA)

15 ft.

23 ft.

9 in.

Backboard

Regulation basketball court.

two purposes: It defines the area in which no player
may remain for more than 3 seconds (unless he is trying to get a rebound). It also establishes the box
alongside which the players of both teams line up
when a foul shot is being attempted.

A center line, known officially as the division line,
but called the halfcourt line, divides the court in half.
It also establishes the 10-second area. A team that
gets possession of the ball in the backcourt must advance out of this half of the court within 10 seconds.

At the center of the court, there's a third 12-foot
circle. This circle is used at the start of the game for
a jump ball.

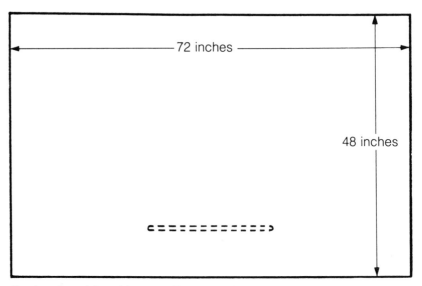

Professional backboard. Below, high school backboard.

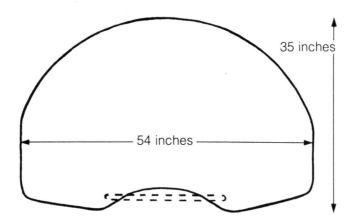

The Ball

The regulation basketball is made of leather or composition material. For boys' and men's games, it weighs between 20 and 22 ounces and is 30 inches in circumference (about 9 inches in diameter).

Girls and women use a basketball that weighs between 18 and 20 ounces and is 29 inches in circumference. This ball is also used by some boys' high school teams.

If you're under 15, your coach may advise you to use the smaller ball. Using a ball that's too big can cause bad shooting and passing habits. When you're bigger and have the correct shooting and passing techniques, you can switch to the bigger ball.

You can tell whether a basketball has the right

In boys' and men's play, the basketball is 30 inches in circumference. Girls and women use a 29-inch ball.

amount of bounce with this test: Drop the ball from a height of 6 feet. It should rebound from 49 to 54 inches off the floor.

Scoring

Since 1894, basketball's scoring system has been as follows:

A field goal is worth 2 points.

A free throw is worth 1 point.

Change came in 1961. That year, the ABL (American Basketball League), a rival to the NBA, was formed. It attracted attention by trying something new: a field goal worth 3 points. Any shot made from beyond an arcing line 25 feet from the basket was worth 3 points. Of course, other field goals still counted as 2 points.

The American Basketball Association, which operated from 1967–68 through 1975–1976, also adopted the 3-point basket. The rule was introduced into NBA competition in 1979–80. The NBA distance for the 3-point arc is 23 feet, 9 inches around the perimeter, and 22 feet in the corners.

Not everyone applauded the 3-point shot at first. Some thought it was simply a gimmick. It took time for teams to get used to it. In the early 1980s, many teams used the 3-pointer only as a desperation shot at the very end of a quarter or as a weapon for making

a quick comeback. In 1979–80, the Atlanta Hawks attempted only 75 3-pointers the entire season. In
1989–90, Michael Jordan *made* 92 3-pointers (on 245
attempts).

Today, most teams average at least ten 3-point shots
in a game. Many teams have set plays designed to
get players open for 3-point shots. During the 1988-
89 season, the New York Knicks attempted 1,147 3-
pointers, becoming the first team ever to try more
than one thousand in a season.

Almost everyone is sold on the 3-point shot today.
For smaller players, it is especially useful. In fact, for
any player skilled as an outside shooter, it is an effective offensive weapon.

The 3-point shot has served to draw defensive players farther from the basket, providing more operating
room for the forwards and pivotmen.

Michael Jordan became enthusiastic about the 3-
pointer during 1989–90. He made more 3-pointers
that season than he did in the three previous seasons
combined. "It wasn't a planned thing," Jordan says.
"It just happened. It makes guys have to play me farther from the basket. If they get up on me, I can go
around them. If they don't, I can take the shot."

The 3-pointer also has psychological value. "It's a
backbreaking thing if you hit it at the right time,"
says Magic Johnson of the Los Angeles Lakers.
"When you're on a roll, in the groove, and you come

The 3-point field goal was first used in college basketball in the season of 1985–86.

down and make a 3-point bomb, you can almost feel the air go out of the other team. It's almost like making a dunk. The crowd gets pumped up, you get pumped up, and the other team kind of sinks."

The 3-point field goal made its debut in men's and women's college basketball in 1985–86. The 3-point arc in college play is 19 feet, 9 inches from the basket. Some critics say the college 3-pointer is too easy, that it's not much more than a regular jump shot. They say the distance should be extended another foot or so.

While the 3-point rule has proved highly successful in both professional and college play, it has not yet been adopted in high school basketball.

4

CRIME AND PUNISHMENT

James Naismith and others continued to tinker with basketball's rules during the late 1800s and early 1900s. Often their efforts focused upon infractions of the rules, called "fouls," and the way in which penalties for fouls were to be assessed.

At first, the penalty for any physical foul—pushing, tripping, hacking, and the others—was very harsh. Any player guilty of two such fouls had to leave the game. His team played one man short until either side scored a goal. Then the man was permitted to return.

This proved too heavy a penalty.

In 1894, three years after Naismith invented basketball, the foul shot was instituted. The value of a foul shot—or free throw—was set at 1 point and a field goal at 2 points, the system used today.

Fouls carry another penalty besides providing the opposition with a free throw. They can also lead to a

player's being disqualified. In high school and college basketball, a player is disqualified upon committing his fifth personal foul. In the NBA, disqualification comes after six personal fouls. Another player takes the place of the disqualified player, who is not permitted to return to the game.

The Officials

Two officials are in charge of a basketball game. They call fouls and violations and indicate successful field goals.

These officials are usually both called referees. Only in professional play, however, are they both officially referees. In college and high school basketball, the official with the most experience is designated the umpire and is in charge of the game.

To call a foul or rule violation, the referee blows a whistle. This halts play and stops the clock. The referee identifies the foul or violation with a hand or arm signal, then enforces the penalty, usually by awarding a free throw.

Other game officials—scorekeepers and timekeepers—sit at a table behind one of the sidelines. One scorekeeper keeps track of the game's official

"A player shall not hold, push, charge into or impede the progress of an opponent," says the rulebook.

scorebook, recording all field goals, free throws, fouls, and timeouts. A player entering the game must first report to this scorekeeper. A second scorekeeper operates the electronic scoreboard.

One of two timekeepers operates the official game clock. He stops the clock whenever an official blows a whistle and restarts it when the official signals him to do so. In professional and college games, a second timekeeper operates the shot clock.

Fouls

Fouls and the foul shots that result decide many games. A certain number of fouls disqualifies a player, putting him on the bench.

There are both personal and technical fouls. A personal foul occurs when a player holds, hacks, pushes, elbows, or charges into an opponent.

The ordinary penalty for a personal foul is one free throw. But if the foul is committed against a player who is shooting at the basket, the penalty is two free throws.

If a player is fouled while shooting and the ball goes in, the field goal counts and the player gets the free throw. He has a chance for a 3-point play.

A technical foul is called for several different violations. These include fighting, unsportsmanlike conduct, and delaying the game. A technical foul can be

"Two shots," a referee signals to an official scorer.

called on a coach or a nonplayer on the bench, as well as on a player on the floor.

When a technical foul is called, no individual is charged with a personal foul. But the opposing team gets one free throw and also possession of the ball out of bounds.

In high school and college play, a player or coach who is called for three technical fouls is disqualified. In the NBA, it takes only two technical fouls for a coach or player to be disqualified.

Team Fouls

It's common for a team that is leading late in a game to abandon its usual offensive tactics and freeze the ball. Players use up the time remaining by passing and dribbling to keep the ball away from the other team. If the opposing team can't get the ball, it can't score, and if it can't score it can't catch up.

Freezing the ball is common in high school basketball. But in college and professional play, where shot clocks are used, a team can freeze the ball for only a limited amount of time.

When one team does attempt a freeze, the coach of the opposing team is likely to tell his players to foul intentionally. By doing so, the trailing team risks giving up 1 point, but has a chance to gain possession after the free throw and then the opportunity of scoring 2 points.

To try to counteract such tactics, rule makers introduced the "team foul." Each personal foul committed by a player is also counted as a team foul.

In high school play, the first four fouls committed by a team in a half carry the standard penalties—one free throw or two. But beginning with the fifth foul, the fouled player is awarded a bonus free throw, a second foul shot to be taken if the first one is successful. This is called a "one-and-one" situation.

In college basketball, one-and-one begins with the

seventh foul a team commits in a half. In the NBA, one-and-one goes into effect with the fifth foul in each quarter. One-and-one also applies when a team commits more than one foul in the last two minutes of a quarter.

The concept of team fouls dates to the 1950s. However, it has done little to reduce tactical fouling in the late stages of a game. When a team feels it *must* get possession of the ball, the intentional foul is still the way to do it.

Violations

Fouls aren't the only reason for a referee to whistle a play stopped. Officials also call other frequent rule violations.

The most common violations result from ball-handling mistakes. A double dribble—that is, the violation that occurs when a player bounces the ball with both hands at one time—is one example. Traveling, taking steps without dribbling when in possession of the ball, is another. The penalty for these and other violations is loss of possession of the ball.

Rule Enforcement

While the rules for high school and college basketball are very similar to the rules for the professional

On a free-throw attempt, after the ball goes up, players on either side of the free-throw lane jockey for advantageous rebound positions.

game, the way in which they are enforced is different. In the pro game, officials tend to be more lenient.

On any given shot in the NBA, there may be six or seven players underneath the basket. The chances are good that they are all taller than 6-foot-6, and most of them weigh 220 or more. As the ball goes up, there are usually plenty of flying arms and elbows.

A foul could be called in the NBA on virtually every shot. But pro officials are tolerant. "They don't call ticky-tacky fouls here," Dennis Johnson of the Celtics once said. "That's one of the first things you notice."

In a high school or college game, if a player travels—takes an extra step—a whistle usually blasts. In the pro ranks, traveling is often greeted with silence, unless it's flagrant.

"The game is the thing," Chuck Daly, coach of the Detroit Pistons, once told *Sports Illustrated*. "The players are performers. Let them perform as well as they can."

Or take palming, a term that refers to an improper dribble, or actually carrying the ball, even if it's for only a fraction of a second. How can a referee call palming in the NBA? Just about every hand is big enough to catch the ball and drop it again during a dribble. The average NBA player can place his index finger on top of the ball and his thumb underneath. When you're dealing with hands that size, it's tough trying to see palming, much less call it.

The 3-second rule, the one that states a player can remain for no longer than 3 seconds in the free-throw lane, is also bent a bit in the pro ranks. Watch a college game on TV. Then watch a pro game. The chances are good that there will be many more calls for 3-second violations in the college game.

Don't NBA players and officials know the rules? Of course they do. But in the pros, the idea is to keep the game going. "In college, the officials try to run the game," says Ken Hudson, a former NBA official and later a television broadcaster. "In the pros, the officials try to control the game. They try to let the players play."

5

THE SKILLS

Basketball is no day at the beach. It puts greater demands on an athlete than does any other sport. You have to be able to shoot accurately. You have to have the ability to pass quickly and deftly. You have to know how to dribble and rebound.

That's not all. You have to be able to run and jump almost without letup, resisting fatigue and absorbing constant hard knocks from defensive players. It's exciting fun, but it's hard work, too.

Shooting

Of all basketball skills, shooting is most important. From the day a player first discovers basketball, he practices mainly by shooting. And why not? Shots put points on the scoreboard. Shots are what win games.

In professional basketball, the best shooters are extremely accurate; they're on target five or six times for every ten shots they take. However, one reason they hit so often is that they shoot only when they're in a good shooting position and within their shooting range. In other words, they not only have to be skilled to be good scorers, they have to be smart.

One-Hand Push Shot—This shot is as basic to basketball as a hoop and a net. It's very similar to the jump shot in the way it's executed. In fact, it's simply the jump shot without the jump. It's the shot almost all players use from the free-throw line.

An advantage of the one-hand push shot, aside from its reliability in shooting fouls, is that it enables you to shoot the ball as soon as you get it. You don't have to jump. You just raise it and fire.

You can also fake the one-hand push shot. When your opponent reacts, you can pull the ball down and drive for the basket.

Ernie Hobbs of Plainfield, New Jersey, is a shooting instructor who works with pro players from time to time. He's called a "shot doctor." When Hobbs is teaching the one-hand push shot, he starts with the feet. He tells players to get "a good comfortable base . . . weight equally distributed on the balls of your feet, your knees bent, your butt out, and your toes pushing down to elevate your body."

Hobbs also stresses the importance of getting the ball properly balanced on the hand. It should balance on the pads of your fingers, he says, not on the heel of your hand.

In addition, Hobbs instructs players on proper arm position. Your elbow should be as high as your shoulder, he points out. "Lift the ball above the shooting eye so that your thumb is somewhere between your eyebrow and your hairline," Hobbs said in *Sports Illustrated*. "That keeps the ball out of your vision."

Larry Bird of the Boston Celtics shoots a picture-perfect one-hand push shot. His left hand is lightly cupped on the side of the ball. When he launches the ball with his right hand, he gives it a quick flick with his wrist. This puts backspin on the ball on its arc to the basket. When the ball hits the backboard or rim, the backspin encourages it to plunge into the net.

The Jump Shot—The jump shot has been basketball's No. 1 offensive weapon since the 1950s. Joe Fulks, who joined the NBA's Philadelphia Warriors in 1946, is credited with being the first pro player to use it. Nicknamed "Jumpin' Joe," Fulks would hustle down the court with the ball, suddenly stop, leap straight up, and shoot the ball one-handed at the top of his jump.

The shot was a smash hit. Fulks, who had played college ball at Murray State (in Murray, Kentucky), led the league in scoring his rookie season, averaging 23.2 points per game, and Philadelphia won the NBA championship.

Larry Bird of the Boston Celtics demonstrates a classic one-hand push shot.

Other players soon began to use the jumper. It wasn't long before the jump shot was the most widely used shot in basketball.

The reason for the jump shot's popularity is easy to understand. It enables you to shoot over the defensive player guarding you, no matter where you hap-

The jump shot enables you to shoot over defenders' upstretched hands. The shooter here is Auburn's Linda Godby.

pen to be on the floor. And you don't *have* to shoot, of course. If, when you're high in the air, you see an open teammate who happens to be closer to the basket than you are, you can pass to him.

Another advantage of the jump shot has to do with being solidly balanced as you shoot. The idea is to launch the ball at the very top of your jump, at the split second that you have gone as high as you are going to go but before you've started to come back down. At that instant, it's almost as if your feet are firmly planted on the court floor.

The Lay-up—The lay-up is a shot that's commonly used at the end of a fast break or when the shooter has a clear path to the basket.

The instruction books say the shot is best executed by pushing off the inside foot (the foot closest to the basket) while hoisting the ball with both hands. At the top of your jump, you extend your shooting arm toward the target and "lay" the ball gently on the backboard.

Lay-ups executed by pros are often highly creative, however, with only a slight resemblance to what the instruction books say. For example, in the reverse lay-up, the ball is flipped in from the far side of the basket after the player has actually passed beneath

Texas's Travis May soars in for a lay-up.

it. There's nothing in the instruction books about the reverse lay-up.

The Free Throw—The shot awarded to a player who is the victim of a foul or other rule violation is called "free" because there can be no defensive interference. The other players, who line up along either side of the free-throw lane, can only watch. A player has 10 seconds in which to shoot a free throw from the moment he is handed the ball.

When Dr. James Naismith was writing the rules of basketball, he set the free-throw line 15 feet from the basket. That distance has stayed the same to this day.

NBA coaches expect their players to hit seven or eight free throws out of every ten attempts. Some players do better than that. In 1989–90, four NBA players each had a free-throw percentage of .900 or better. Larry Bird, with a .930 percentage, led the league. That's only .070 from perfection.

To become a better free-throw shooter, Bird advises, set goals. Shoot forty or fifty practice free throws every day, he says. Keep track of how many you make and never stop trying to improve your percentage. And concentrate when you practice. Make believe each shot is the one that's going to win your team the world championship.

Detroit's Bill Laimbeer sends up a free throw.

Almost all players use the one-hand push shot in shooting free throws. But once in a while a player comes along who tosses the ball up underhand using both hands. One advantage of this style is that it enables you to put a great deal of backspin on the ball. If it hits the back of the rim or the backboard, it usually plunges downward toward the basket. Rick Barry of the Golden State Warriors, pro basketball's best foul shooter in the 1970s, used the underhand style.

The Hook Shot—Of all the many different shots in basketball, the hook shot is the most difficult to learn. You begin the shot with your back to the basket, holding the ball in one hand away from your body. Then, with your arm fully extended, you sweep the ball toward the basket over your head. Because your back is to the player who's defending you as you shoot, the ball is almost impossible to block.

However, it is not easy to be accurate with the hook shot. Players use it primarily when they're close to the basket.

Kareem Abdul-Jabbar, who stands 7-foot-2, relied on a variation of the hook shot in which the ball seemed to have been delivered from the heavens. It was called the "skyhook." It's doubtful whether anyone ever blocked Kareem's skyhook. Larry Bird has a running hook shot that is almost as unstoppable.

The Dunk—"I'm sure that when James Naismith hung up that first peach basket," basketball Hall of

Kareem Abdul-Jabbar's skyhook was practically unstoppable.

Famer Bob Cousy once noted, "it was with the idea that people would be shooting at it and not down through it." What Cousy was referring to, of course, was the dunk shot, a field goal made by slamming the ball through the basket from above the rim.

Not every player can execute a dunk. To pull it off, you must have greater than average height, extraordinary jumping ability, or both.

The dunk shot has become much more than a means of scoring 2 points. It's also a way of intimidating an opponent, of psyching him out. "It's an 'in-your-face' thing," one NBA player explains.

Even more than that, a dunk is a way of rousing the fans. A sharp pass gets nods of approval; a high-arching 3-pointer earns cheers and applause. But a backward, over-the-head, rim-rattling dunk brings the spectators to their feet screaming.

The first NBA player to feature the dunk was Gus Johnson, who joined the Baltimore Bullets in 1963. "Johnson was the first guy who could really fly," Red Auerbach, the Celtic coaching great, once recalled. "He was awesome."

Seven-footer Wilt Chamberlain, or the "Big Dipper," as he liked to be called, was another celebrated dunker. During his NBA career, which spanned the seasons from 1959–60 through 1972–73, many of Chamberlain's most memorable dunks came in two situations: when he wanted to teach an opponent a lesson, and when he was trying to nail down a scoring record.

One of the most noted of Wilt's "lessons" was delivered to Johnny Kerr, a star for the Syracuse Nationals in the 1960s. After Kerr had made Chamberlain look bad on a play, Kerr was on the receiving end of a fearsome dunk on each of Wilt's next four trips down the court. On the fourth, Chamberlain stuffed the ball so hard that it shot through the net and struck Kerr on the foot, injuring his toe.

Today, Chamberlain is rightly regarded as one of basketball's all-time greats. (He is profiled on page 135.) But throughout his career he had one failing: he could not shoot free throws with any consistency. To overcome this weakness, Wilt as a high-school player, tried dunking them. While palming the ball, he would take two giant steps from behind the free-throw line and then spring toward the basket. Before either foot touched the floor, he would jam the ball through the hoop.

It's no accident that you've never seen a free throw made in this fashion. The NCAA banned the practice in 1955, the same year Chamberlain entered college.

The rule makers banned all dunking from high school and college basketball from the 1968–69 to the 1975–76 basketball seasons. During this time, pro dunking zoomed in popularity.

In 1967, the American Basketball Association, a ri-

Reggie Miller of the Indiana Pacers dunks one.

val to the NBA, played its first season. To attract fans, the league encouraged a wide-open, more colorful style of play. In the ABA, the dunk shot was raised to an art form. While playing for the ABA's Pittsburgh Pipers, Charlie "Helicopter" Hentz actually broke two backboards in one game with his enthusiastic dunks.

The ABA's Virginia Squires team was the launching pad for the career of Julius Erving, the fabled "Dr. J," who joined it in 1971. The Doctor (who is profiled beginning on page 128) lifted the dunk shot to new heights. Leaping dunks from as far away as the foul line were Erving's specialty. He personalized each one. Some he jammed in with his tomahawk slam; others, with his back to the basket.

"The no-dunking rule came in my senior year in high school," Julius once recalled, "so I hadn't been allowed to slam for four years. At first, I couldn't get enough of it." A fearsome dunk over Kareem Abdul-Jabbar in the NBA All-Star Game in 1976 helped Erving establish himself in that league.

But there's a problem with the dunk, one that first became apparent in the 1980s and by the beginning of the 1990s was painfully obvious—there was too much dunking.

Some dunks are OK; others aren't. There's nothing wrong when a player who's 6-foot-10 or so slams the ball through; it may be the highest-percentage shot he has at the time. It's the showoff dunks—such as when a 6-footer on a breakaway turns what should be a simple lay-up into a circus move, slamming in a one-hander while turning himself into a corkscrew—that have alarmed the critics.

During a game between Nebraska and Kansas in 1988, Kansas guard Otis Livingston, barely 6 feet tall, got the ball with no one between himself and the basket. Rather than attempt an easy lay-up, Livingston went soaring into the air to try a one-handed sweep slam. He missed; the ball rebounded off the heel of the rim.

Nebraska eventually won the game on a last-second field goal. Livingston's blown shot wasn't the only reason that Kansas lost. There were other misses. But these had to do with poor execution or alert defensive play. Livingston's miss could be blamed only on a lapse in discipline.

No one is saying that the dunk shot should be outlawed, as it once was. There are exceptions, of course, but any player who hasn't yet reached 6-foot-6 should think carefully before attempting one.

Passing

Passes are what make the offense work. Sharp passing can split a zone defense apart. An effective offensive strategy is to bounce passes into the corner, stretching the defense, then suddenly whip the ball into the weakened middle. Good passes are what enable a team to penetrate a man-to-man defense.

Passes are more important in college basketball than ever before. That's because the 3-point shot, introduced in 1985, has opened up the game by forcing offenses to spread out. As a result, defenses have also had to stretch out. The result is a greater emphasis on passing.

When Pete Carril, Princeton head coach during the late 1980s, was evaluating a high school prospect, one of the first things he would ask about the boy was, "Can he see?" What Carril meant was, "Can he pass?" To Carril, as to many other coaches, no basketball skill is more important than passing.

Any time you pass the ball, you should try to deliver it crisply, confidently. Snap your wrists. You want to get the ball where it's going as fast as possible.

Try faking before you pass. Look away from your target before you release the ball. After you pass, move. Cut for the basket and look for a return pass. Get set for a rebound. Set a pick. There are many things you can do offensively even after you have passed the ball.

There are many different kinds of passes. The *two-hand chest pass* is the simplest, quickest, and most widely used. To execute this pass, you hold the ball

chest high, gripping it on each side. When you release the ball, you step in the direction of the pass
and snap your wrists.

The chest pass is often used to get the ball upcourt
fast. It's also used in working the ball around the perimeter of a defense. There's no better way to get the
ball to an unobstructed target.

The *bounce pass* is executed in almost the same
way as the chest pass. The difference is that you aim
at a spot on the floor instead of targeting on a teammate. The bounce pass is often used to get the ball
to a receiver who's cutting through heavy traffic. But
be careful; the bounce pass is easier than any other
to intercept.

The *overhead pass* is just what its name implies—a
pass made with the ball above your head. You snap
your wrists forward as you release the ball.

The *baseball pass* is a long-range pass. You bring
the ball back on your throwing side, holding it in one
hand just above shoulder level. You push off from
your rear foot as you whip the ball forward, releasing
it with a snap of the wrist. The process is similar to
the way in which a quarterback throws a football.
Maybe this pass should be called the "football pass."

The *lob pass* is made with a baseball throw or two-

*Double-teamed by a pair of Timberwolves, Joe Barry Carroll of
the Denver Nuggets uses an overhead pass to get the ball away.*

handed. The idea is to get the ball over the defense, targeting on one of your team's big men. The lob pass is often used to lead a player so he can make the catch without breaking stride and lay the ball up.

There is also the hook pass and jump pass (executed in much the same fashion as the hook shot and jump shot). The behind-the-back pass is often used when you are so tightly boxed in by opposing players you have no other way to get the ball to a teammate. But be careful with fancy passes. A turnover, a loss of possession, is a terrible thing.

Dribbling

A player is not permitted to walk or run with the ball unless he dribbles it—that is, bounces it. Watch a pro player dribble. Notice that he dribbles with his head up and his eyes looking straight ahead. A player who dribbles with his head down isn't able to see where he's going. And he can't see teammates who are open for passes.

Dribbling is the way a player moves the ball without passing it. But there is no reason for a player to dribble if he can pass or shoot.

Larry Bird once put it in these terms: "The shot is your 'big gun.' The pass is your 'spear,' and the dribble is your 'knife.' You need to choose your best weapon for each situation."

When you're dribbling and tightly guarded, you must protect the ball. This is Derek Harper of the Dallas Mavericks.

What Bird meant was that when you have a good shot, take it. If you can't shoot but you spot an open man, then pass. Use your "knife"—your dribble, that is—only when you're not able to shoot or pass.

Rebounding

Rebounding—getting the ball as it comes off the backboard or rim—is another essential skill, as vital to a team's success as passing and shooting. A team that can't control the boards seldom wins.

Actually, there are two types of rebounding—offensive and defensive. An offensive rebound occurs when a player on the shooter's team reaches the ball. Defensive rebounds are picked up by the nonshooting team.

Rebounding is never any picnic. Often there are three or four players going up for the ball at the same time. You may get elbowed, shoved, or bumped. Rebounding requires strength and quickness—and a fair amount of courage.

Although it sometimes looks like a circus beneath the boards when a shot goes up, there is organization to rebounding. Most teams attempt to reach rebounds by forming a protective triangle around the basket. One player takes up a position in the middle of the foul lane. The other two are in closer on either side of the lane. When a shot is made, all three players turn to face the rim. The player that's closest to the rebound leaps for it.

Offensive rebounding is the roughest. That's because the team shooting the ball is usually not as well positioned for rebounds as the defensive team. The

A key to success in offensive rebounding is anticipating where the ball is heading. Sleepy Floyd of the Houston Rockets grabs the rebound here.

players on offense have to first get past the opposition in order to get to the rebounding ball. And the defensive players are trying to box out their opponents—that is, each is attempting to position his body between an offensive player and the ball.

As an offensive rebounder, always try to anticipate where the ball is heading. You know your teammates; you know their shooting habits. When a teammate gets set to shoot, you should head for a likely rebound position.

If you're the shooter, follow your shot. You know better than anyone else how the ball will rebound.

If you grab the ball near the basket, go right up with it again. If you can't get both hands on the ball, at least try to tap it back up to keep the ball alive. Or look for a chance to tap it to a teammate.

If a defensive player tries to block your path to the basket, you can use a body fake to get around him. Or you can try running out of bounds and then come back to establish position under the basket. There's nothing illegal about going out of bounds without the ball.

On defense, the first rule of rebounding is to keep the offensive player from going to the basket. You do this by boxing out (also called blocking out).

The key to boxing out effectively is being in a good defensive position—that is, positioned between your opponent and the basket—before the shot goes up.

As soon as the ball is in the air, pivot around so you face the basket. Keep your feet well apart; stay low. As you watch the ball, take a couple of short steps back so your buttocks are jammed into your opponent. Keep your arms out.

All the time, watch the path of the ball. If it rebounds to within your reach, grab it. Hold it close to your body. Stick out your elbows.

Now you're an offensive player. Look for a teammate to whom you can pass. If possible, get the ball to the player on your team who is the farthest downcourt. Rebounds are what trigger fast breaks.

Jumping

Some basketball players can jump out of the gym. Darrell Griffith of the University of Louisville, who later played for the Utah Jazz, once soared 48 inches—that's four feet!—in a jump-and-reach drill. Other players, however, can scarcely get off the floor.

How high can you jump? You can measure your jumping height with what is called a jump differential, which is the difference between your reach flat-footed and the point you can reach after a one-step leap.

Here's how it works: Stand next to a wall and reach up with a piece of tape. Stick the tape as high up on the wall as you can without getting up on your toes.

Now take another piece of tape. After taking one step, jump as high as you can and slap the second piece of tape onto the wall. Measure the difference between the two pieces of tape. That's your jump differential.

For boys, the jump differential is usually between 16 and 19 inches. For girls, it's 14 to 17 inches. A boy with a differential of greater than 23 inches is a superior jumper. The same can be said of a girl with a differential of more than 20 inches.

As a rule, a leap of one-third or more of one's height is extraordinary. If you stand 5-foot-4—64 inches, that is—consider a leap of 21 to 22 inches to be remarkable.

Some basketball players are such exceptional leapers that these standards of excellence don't apply to them. Take Anthony "Spud" Webb of the Atlanta Hawks. Webb, at 5-feet-7, is the smallest player in the NBA. Yet he is one of the league's best jumpers.

Webb once won the NBA's Slam Dunk Championship, outdueling teammate Dominique Wilkins in the finals. Wilkins is 6-feet-7. Webb won not only because of the spectacular quality and tremendous variety of his dunks, but also because of his extraordinary jumping ability on shot after shot.

Spud has been interviewed many times about his ability to jump. "I never really worked on it," he says. "It's a God-given talent."

Spud Webb can jump high, but he's more valued for his quickness and ability to penetrate.

Recalling the summer before his senior year of high school, he once said: "I had been trying to dunk it hundreds of times, and I finally got one." Spud was 5-foot-4 at the time.

Webb has said he probably would never have played in the NBA were it not for his jumping prowess. He was being modest when he said that. In fact, his quickness and ability to penetrate are more valuable than his ability to get up into the air.

How important is jumping ability in basketball? Some experts believe it is overrated. Says Jack Ramsey, former coach of the Portland Trailblazers: "It's spectacular, and it gets reaction from the fans, but it's not a dominating factor."

For example, jumping has little to do with being a successful rebounder, many experts say. What counts is positioning. The same is true when it comes to scoring. Getting up in the air is important to dunking, but a player must have a variety of other skills to put the ball in the basket consistently.

Larry Bird is not a good jumper. Neither is Magic Johnson.

"It's an asset," Ramsey says, "but it's not what makes a player good."

6

CENTERS, FORWARDS, GUARDS

A basketball team has a center, two guards, and two forwards on the court at all times. They play both offense and defense. Because possession of the ball can change in a split second, players have to be alert to switch from offense to defense and back again.

Players can move anywhere on the court at any time, no matter what position they play. But guards, who are responsible for bringing the ball up the court and starting plays, normally play farther from the basket than the center or the forwards. As you might expect, guards are usually a team's best ball handlers.

Forwards normally play on either side of the free-throw lane near the basket. They're usually taller, heavier, and stronger than the guards.

In the NBA, the five-player team is part of a squad that is limited to twelve players. In high school basketball, fifteen players are permitted on the full squad. The nonstarters are substitutes—other guards, forwards, and centers who are ready to enter the game to replace a player who needs rest or is injured.

"Free" substitution is permitted in basketball. This means that players can leave and reenter the game any number of times. It's not like baseball, where a player who has been replaced may not reenter the game.

Playing Center

When Bill Russell, often called the greatest center in basketball history, was taking up his duties as the new coach of the NBA's Sacramento Kings in 1987, he had three candidates for the position at which he once starred. LaSalle Thompson was a better-than-average shooter and rebounder, but was only 6-foot-10. There were forwards in the league who were taller than that.

Jawann Oldham, at 7 feet, was tall enough and very agile, but his offensive skills needed sharpening. Joe Kleine played the post efficiently, he could pass, and he could shoot. But Kleine lacked mobility.

Russell was puzzled. "They're so different," he said, "it's hard to believe they play the same position."

It's easy to understand why Russell was confused. He had joined the Celtics in 1956 and played throughout the 1960s (helping to lead the team to eleven NBA titles in thirteen seasons). In Russell's day, the center's role was clearly defined. On virtually every team, the center was the most important player on the team, and the tallest. He played near the basket—that is, he "posted up," relaying passes to his teammates and taking shots himself.

Not only was the center the focal point of the team's offense, he was the team's No. 1 rebounder. He also excelled at stopping or deflecting shots—that is, shot blocking.

It's different nowadays. Centers are much more versatile. Whereas the center used to play with his back to the basket, he now often faces the basket. He'll move to the outside to take a 15- or 16-foot jumper or drive in for a lay-up. In the 1990s, a center can even be seen leading a fast break.

Akeem Olajuwon of the Houston Rockets is the pro game's dominant center. He has tremendous size—he's 7-feet tall—and strength. He is quick and has explosive jumping ability. He excels in scoring, rebounds, blocked shots, and steals, and he has a deceptive spin-and-drive move. He can, it seems, score about anytime he wants to. A player can't be more dominant than that.

Bill Laimbeer, center for the Detroit Pistons, NBA champions in 1988–89 and again in 1989–90, is another example of the change in the status of centers. Laimbeer is neither a shot blocker nor an inside

Robert Parrish (00) has had a long career as a standout center for the Celtics.

scorer. Rather, he's a rugged defensive player and deadly shooter from the outside.

Hall of Famer George Mikan, basketball's first great center, marvels at what the center position has become. "When I played, it was the center's duty to be within ten feet of the basket," he once recalled. "The only time I would shoot from the outside was in practice, and then it was only when we were shooting for 'milkshakes.'"

Playing Forward

Centers used to be able to dominate the game simply because they were taller than everybody else. Not anymore. Now forwards are big, too.

Charles Oakley of the New York Knicks is 6-foot-9. Boston's Kevin McHale is 6-foot-10. Atlanta's Kevin Willis is a 7-footer. All are forwards. If they had played fifteen years ago, they would have been centers.

Not only are forwards taller than they used to be, they're much more versatile. They get the ball in the post area—that is, near the free-throw lane. They have taken over what used to be the center's chief role.

Another big difference is that many of today's forwards don't hesitate to go up for rebounds. There were some exceptions, of course, but in basketball's early days forwards rebounded about as often as they sold soft drinks at halftime.

Not only do forwards do everything, however. The position has become specialized. There are "power" forwards and "small" forwards.

The power forward position came about as a result of the rapid expansion that took place in the NBA during the late 1960s and early 1970s. There were nine NBA teams in 1965–66. By 1970–71, there were seventeen. What developed was a shortage of centers—talented players who could post up, rebound, and block shots.

Consequently, forwards on many teams were called upon to play the post and take over some of the center's rebounding and shot-blocking responsibilities. These players were the first power forwards. One example was Paul Silas of the Boston Celtics, who played a key role when Boston won NBA championships in 1973–74 and 1975–76.

Creative, a team player, Danny Manning is a power forward for the Los Angeles Clippers.

Other forwards were called upon to be scorers. These players came to be known as small forwards.

One of the first small forwards was Julius Erving, Dr. J, who crossed over from the ABA to the NBA in 1976. At 6-foot-7 and 205 pounds, Erving combined the size and strength of a big man with the quickness of a guard. His greatest skill was in driving to the basket, weaving his way through the defense or soaring over it, creating moves as needed.

The term "small forward" is not a good one. It confuses things, because there are small forwards who are tall. Karl Malone, small forward for the Utah Jazz, is 6-foot-9.

And there are small forwards who sometimes cross over to the guard positions. Chris Mullin of the Golden State Warriors and Paul Pressy of the San Antonio Spurs are two examples. Mullin sometimes plays shooting guard; Pressy also plays point guard.

The legendary Larry Bird was a small forward for the Boston Celtics. While Bird was an exceptional shooter and rebounder, he lacked the quickness and jumping ability most people expect of a forward. The reason he was called a small forward was simply that he wasn't the Celtics' power forward. That position had long been held by Kevin McHale, known for his talent in the low post—close to the basket, that is.

While there may be confusion about the small-forward position and the terminology used to describe

James Worthy (right), who's 6-feet-9, is a small forward for the Los Angeles Lakers.

it, no one disputes its importance. Besides Larry Bird, NBA small forwards have included the Atlanta Hawks' Dominique Wilkins, the Los Angeles Lakers' James Worthy, and the Philadelphia 76ers' Charles Barkley. These players have been among the biggest stars in the NBA in recent years. When they do well, their teams usually do well.

The Guards

During the past decade or so, the position of guard has become specialized. Today, guards are either shooting guards or point guards.

The point guard came into prominence as players got quicker and defenses better. Just moving the ball up the court was getting harder and harder. What good was it to have a 7-footer planted under the basket if his team couldn't get the ball to him?

That's where the point guard comes in. The point guard's job is to act as the team's chief ball handler. He dribbles the ball up the court. Then, from the area above the free-throw circle, he directs the team's offense. The point guard also has to be a skilled shooter, able to hit the 20- to 25-foot jump shot.

According to Al McGuire, basketball analyst for NBC, the first thing to look for in a point guard is quickness. "He's got to be a bit of a waterbug," says McGuire. "But he's got to have a head, too. He's

As Chicago's shooting guard, tough, solid John Paxson complements Michael Jordan.

your coach on the floor—picking up the tempo when you're behind and putting it in the refrigerator when you're ahead."

A point guard has to be an unselfish player, too, willing to give up the ball when he should. It's the point guard's role to make other players look good. A point guard who yearns to see his name in the headlines should consider playing another position.

There are no strict height requirements for being a guard. In high school or college ball, guards are usually the smallest players on the court.

That's also true in the NBA. However pro guards are not small by everyday standards; they're anything but. Most are at least 6-foot-4, and they keep getting bigger. In fact, the "other" guard, the shooting guard, is also known as the tall guard or the big guard.

Darrell Walker is a hustling, rebounding point guard for the Bullets.

"More than anything else, the big guard has evolved because the league has gotten so big," explains Rick Sund, director of player personnel for the Dallas Mavericks. "By that I mean, players who would have been forwards ten years ago are now forced to play guard."

Examples are talented players such as the Chicago Bulls' Michael Jordan, who's 6-foot-6, the Los Angeles Lakers' Magic Johnson (6-foot-9), and the Portland Trail Blazers' Clyde Drexler (6-foot-3).

Players like these can win games almost single-handedly. Each of them takes smaller defensive players close to the basket and either shoots over them or uses his strength to get easy shots. Each uses his speed and quickness to outdrive opponents to the basket. Jordan, Johnson, and the others are capable of a "triple double"—hitting double figures in points, assists, and rebounds—on any given night.

Since a good part of this chapter has been concerned with the subject of height in basketball, it is interesting to know who was the tallest player on record. According to the *Guinness Book of World Records*, that honor goes to Suleiman Ali Nashnash, who played for the Libyan national team in 1962. Nineteen years old at the time, Ali Nashnash was exactly 8 feet tall.

The tallest woman player on record is Alexsandr Sizonenko, a member of the team representing the Soviet Union in the 1972 Olympic Games. She stood 7-foot-2 and weighed 281 pounds. With Sizonenko playing center, the Soviet women were heavily favored to win the basketball gold medal—and they did.

7

OFFENSE VS. DEFENSE

It is near the end of the fourth quarter of a game at Madison Square Garden. The New York Knicks are playing the Boston Celtics. The Celtics are ahead, but the Knicks are starting to catch up.

Larry Bird, the Celtics' star forward, calls a time-out. A few minutes later, Bird, without the ball and guarded by Johnny Newman, comes around a pick set by Robert Parrish, the Celtics' center. Bird stops at the side of the basket.

Dennis Johnson, a veteran guard for the Celtics, has the ball near the foul line. Bird looks at Johnson and points to the far corner. It's as if he's saying, that's where you should pass the ball.

Johnson looks to where Bird is pointing. So does Johnny Newman, over his shoulder. As he does, Johnson hits Bird with a quick pass. As Newman turns back around, he watches Bird put in an easy lay-up.

That play is typical of what most teams try to do on offense—get the ball to the open man.

Offensive Styles

Teams have different ways in which they seek to accomplish their offensive goals. Some, for example, rely upon an offense that is based on a few basic formations and from which certain variations flow. They like to simply move the ball and see what happens. These teams are exciting and unpredictable. Other teams run more of a disciplined offense. Players on these teams are always getting drilled in X's and O's.

Some teams emphasize rapid ball movement, with plenty of motion, cutting, and passing. Other teams prefer to get things done slowly and carefully. They often score by hitting from the outside. They attempt 3-point field goals with regularity.

Many coaches stress defense as a way to generate offense. They run a tough, tight defense, a pressure defense. They seek to choke offensive life out of their opponents. At the same time, these teams look to start rallies with steals or traps—that is, by legally taking the ball away from an opponent or double-teaming the opponent with the ball.

In developing a team's attack, a coach doesn't always have complete freedom. His offense has to match the talents of the players he happens to have.

The Houston Rockets, for example, like to fast-break, taking advantage of Akeem Olajuwon's skills as a rebounder and shot blocker. The New York Knicks' offense often concentrates on getting the ball to Patrick Ewing, who is Mr. Everything for his team.

Offensive Tactics

Some teams like to use the center or a forward as the focal point of the team's attack. This player will take up a position close to the basket, called a low post, or near the foul line, the high post. Once he posts up, the pivotman, as he's often called, takes passes and looks to hit an open man or shoot. He also keeps alert for rebounds.

A high post gives a team's forwards and guards more opportunity to maneuver under the basket. The high-post pivotman usually passes a great deal. A low post is best suited for a pivotman who's effective with a jumper or hook shot.

The fast break is a very common offensive tactic. A team seeks to get the ball downcourt as quickly as possible, to a player who has gotten ahead of the defense.

The give-and-go is another common offensive maneuver. It involves only two players. One passes the ball to the other, then cuts to an open area for a re-

When it works, a fast break ends like this, with defensive players trailing a forward who goes in for a lay-up.

turn pass. It's a simple maneuver, but it takes near-perfect timing.

Screens and picks are other common offensive tactics. A screening player positions his body so it acts as a barrier, or "screen," from behind which the player with the ball can shoot.

A pick is similar to a screen. One player takes advantage of a block set by a teammate to move to the basket with the ball or cut to an open area to get a pass.

On Defense

There are two basic types of defense in basketball. One is man-to-man and the other is zone.

In a man-to-man defense, each player is assigned to guard a particular opponent. (Even women's teams call it "man-to-man.") The defensive player follows his assignment all over the floor throughout the game.

In a zone defense, each player covers a particular area of the court, guarding any opponent who enters that "zone." The zone defense is not permitted in the NBA. It is thought to slow down the game needlessly.

Every man-to-man defense uses some zone principles, and every zone defense has some man-to-man features. For example, in a man-to-man, players must always be aware of the ball's location. In a zone, players have to be alert and well balanced, staying between the man being guarded and the ball, making it as difficult as possible for him to receive a pass.

Each player in a man-to-man defense has to be determined and aggressive. There's no room for error.

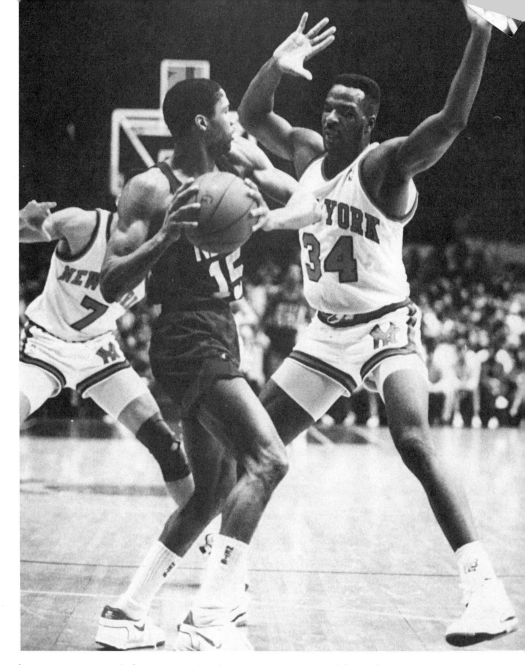

In man-to-man defense, each player has to cover his or her opponent like a coat of paint. Charles Oakley of the Knicks is the defender here.

Whether playing man-to-man or zone, it's vital to keep alert, obstructing passes whenever possible. Traci Thirdgill demonstrates.

If there is a weak defensive player, the offensive team can create a mismatch so as to take advantage of this weakness. But a defensive team employing a zone defense can compensate for a weakness by having other players help out.

The zone has other advantages. For example, it's usually difficult for a team to work the ball close to the basket against a zone. That's because the defensive players are concentrating on the ball no matter where it happens to be, and passing into the zone can be risky. Even if an offensive team succeeds in penetrating a zone, getting a shot off underneath is difficult.

There are two basic methods of playing against a zone. The simplest is not to attempt to penetrate, but instead to shoot over the zone from far out. Of course, the offensive team must have a shooter who's accurate from outside for this strategy to be effective.

Another tactic is to try to "overload" the zone. The ball is worked to one side of the zone until a player can dart through from the opposite side for a pass.

Defensive Tactics

Besides using zone and man-to-man defenses, teams also employ presses, sags, and switches as defensive tactics.

When a team presses, players make a maximum ef-

Some teams put an emphasis on defense. Here Texas's Lance Blanks and Travis Mays trap SMU's Eric Longino.

fort to guard closely. The idea is to force a turn-over—a bad pass or a muffed dribble—which can lead to an interception or a steal.

A full-court press is one in which the tight guarding starts at the far end of the court, the moment the opposing team puts the ball in play. A half-court press begins near the halfcourt line.

Sagging defenses are commonly used when the opposition has a strong center or forward who is a threat to score whenever he gets close to the basket. The defensive center plays between his man and the basket. His teammates "drop off" the men they are guarding to help him out. This makes it difficult for the opposition to get the ball to the dangerous scorer.

Switching is common with man-to-man defenses. Sometimes, when a pair of offensive players cross, it's easier for the defensive players guarding them to switch assignments than it is to stay with their original assignments.

8

BASKETBALL COMPETITION

Nothing stirs the nation's basketball fans as does the NCAA (National Collegiate Athletic Association) tournament, held in March each year. That's when sixty-four college teams set out on a three-week journey that leads to the Final Four and then the national championship. It's sometimes called "March Madness."

Sellout crowds fill the big arenas where the finals are held. Millions more watch on national television.

In the NCAA women's tournament, thirty-two teams compete. In 1990, record crowds turned out to watch the women's finals and semifinals.

College Competition

Approximately 750 schools in the NCAA sponsor men's basketball; 550 schools sponsor women's teams. Competition and scheduling are based on divisions.

Teams from schools with the largest enrollments compete in Division I. Smaller schools make up Division II and Division III.

About 500 other colleges and universities belong to the National Association of Intercollegiate Athletics (NAIA). Like NCAA member schools, NAIA schools sponsor both men's and women's basketball competition.

In an intraconference contest, Louisiana Tech, of the America South Conference, faces Auburn, representing the Southeastern Conference.

Most of the colleges and universities in the NCAA and NAIA belong to one of the more than one hundred college conferences. A conference, made up of teams in the same geographical area, is similar to a league or association. Teams in the same conference play one another during the season; they also play teams outside the conference, but less frequently.

According to rules set down by the NCAA, the college basketball season begins on the Friday after Thanksgiving. College teams are not permitted to play more than 28 games during a season, not counting tournament competition. A team that enters postseason tournaments may end up playing as many as 37 or 38 games.

For the players, it's a long season. It actually begins early in September with the first day of school, when players start working on conditioning. Formal practice sessions begin in mid-October. Many colleges schedule practices seven days a week. Tournament play can stretch the season deep into March.

The NCAA's basketball champions are determined by a round of tournaments at the end of the regular season. Sixty-four teams are chosen to compete in the Division I tournament. Many of these teams are conference champions.

There are also tournaments for Division II and Division III schools. The NAIA holds its own tournament.

St. John's meets Rutgers in the Big East Conference.

Still another postseason tournament is sponsored by the Metropolitan Intercollegiate Basketball Association of New York. It's the National Invitation Tournament, the NIT. It draws Division I teams from throughout the United States.

MAJOR COLLEGE BASKETBALL CONFERENCES

ATLANTIC COAST

Clemson Tigers
Duke Blue Devils
Florida Gators
Georgia Tech Yellow Jackets
Maryland Terrapins
North Carolina State
  Wolfpack
North Carolina Tar Heels
Virginia Cavaliers

BIG EAST

Boston College Eagles
Connecticut Huskies
Georgetown Hoyas
Miami Hurricanes
Pittsburgh Panthers
Providence Friars
St. John's Redmen
Seton Hall Pirates
Syracuse Orangemen
Villanova Wildcats

BIG EIGHT

Colorado Buffaloes
Iowa State Cyclones
Kansas Jayhawks
Kansas State Wildcats
Missouri Tigers
Nebraska Cornhuskers
Oklahoma Sooners
Oklahoma State Cowboys

BIG TEN

Illinois Fighting Illini
Indiana Hoosiers
Iowa Hawkeyes
Michigan State Spartans
Michigan Wolverines
Minnesota Golden Gophers
Northwestern Wildcats
Ohio State Buckeyes
Penn State Nittany Lions
Purdue Boilermakers
Wisconsin Badgers

However, the NIT and all other college tournaments are overshadowed by the NCAA's Division I championships. The first stage in the event is to determine the sixteen regional champions, sometimes called the "Sweet Sixteen." For many teams, reaching this plateau is the measure of a successful season.

The four finalists, the "Final Four," meet in a doubleheader to decide which teams will battle it out for the title. Many enthusiasts consider this to be the most exciting day of the sporting year.

IVY LEAGUE	PAC-10
Brown Bears	Arizona State Sun Devils
Columbia Lions	Arizona Wildcats
Cornell Big Red	California Golden Bears
Dartmouth Big Green	Oregon Ducks
Harvard Crimson	Oregon State Beavers
Pennsylvania Quakers	Southern California Trojans
Princeton Tigers	Stanford Cardinals
Yale Bulldogs	UCLA Bruins
	Washington Huskies
	Washington State Cougars

SOUTHEASTERN	
	SOUTHWEST
Alabama Crimson Tide	
Arkansas Razorbacks	Baylor Bears
Auburn Tigers	Houston Cougars
Florida Gators	Rice Owls
Georgia Bulldogs	Southern Methodist
Kentucky Wildcats	Mustangs
LSU Tigers	Texas A&M Aggies
Mississippi Rebels	Texas Christian Horned
Mississippi State Bulldogs	Frogs
Tennessee Volunteers	Texas Longhorns
Vanderbilt Commodores	Texas Tech Red Raiders

Forty-eight hours later, the two finalists meet in the deciding game. It's joy for one team and its fans, heartbreak for the other.

Major upsets usually add to the drama. In 1988, the Kansas Jayhawks captured the championship by whipping an Oklahoma team that was supposed to blow them away. For real shock value, however, no tournament final has been able to match Villanova's victory over heavily favored Georgetown in 1985. That game put a sad finish to the college career of

Action in the Southwest Conference: Texas vs. Texas A & M.

Patrick Ewing, who would go on to star for the New York Knicks.

The first NCAA postseason tournament took place in 1939. Held at Patten Gymnasium on the campus of Northwestern University in Evanston, Illinois, the tournament consisted of eight teams and attracted 15,025 spectators for its five dates.

In the final, Oregon met Ohio State. Oregon won, 46–43.

Professional Competition

Professional basketball means the National Basketball Association. The NBA consists of 27 teams, which are grouped into two conferences and four divisions. Each team plays an 82-game schedule that begins early in November.

One highlight of the season is the NBA All-Star Weekend, staged in February. Festivities include appearances by pro stars of the past, a slam-dunk competition, and a contest in which some of the game's finest marksmen shoot it out from 3-point range. Last, two dozen of the game's most accomplished players compete in the All-Star Game.

In April, after the regular season has ended and the champions in each division have been decided, it's playoff time. Sixteen teams qualify for postseason play. Four of the playoff berths go to the division champions, and the remaining spots to the six teams in each conference that compiled the best record during the regular season.

In the first round of the playoffs, each series is con-

NATIONAL BASKETBALL ASSOCIATION

EASTERN CONFERENCE

Atlantic Coast

Boston Celtics
New Jersey Nets
New York Knickerbockers
Philadelphia 76ers
Washington Bullets
Miami Heat

Central Division

Atlanta Hawks
Chicago Bulls
Cleveland Cavaliers
Detroit Pistons
Indiana Pacers
Milwaukee Bucks
Charlotte Hornets

WESTERN CONFERENCE

Midwest

Dallas Mavericks
Denver Nuggets
Houston Rockets
San Antonio Spurs
Utah Jazz
Minnesota Timberwolves
Orlando Magic

Pacific Division

Golden State Warriors
Los Angeles Clippers
Los Angeles Lakers
Phoenix Suns
Portland Trail Blazers
Sacramento Kings
Seattle Supersonics

In the NBA All-Star Game, stars of the Eastern Conference face those representing the Western Conference. Here, Kareem Abdul-Jabbar tunes up for one of his ten All-Star appearances.

ducted on a best-of-five basis. In all succeeding series, it's best-of-seven.

Playoff competition lasts several weeks. The NBA champion is not crowned until June.

Many high school basketball players want to become pro stars one day. What are their chances? Not very good, according to statistics. Only about one in every 10,000 high school players get to play in the NBA. Your chances of becoming an astronaut are probably better.

9

THE BEST

Choosing the best players from basketball's earliest days to the present is no easy task. What do you use as a yardstick? Statistics alone are not always reliable. They can give a wrong impression.

Scoring ability, defensive talents, and play-making are vital, of course. And the players featured in this chapter have each excelled in one or more of those areas.

One other standard of comparison is important. The players profiled here have each had a deep influence upon the game. They've been responsible for tactical breakthroughs on offense or defense—or both. They've taken the game into new territory. There's no greater achievement.

Michael Jordan

When sportswriters were casting their ballots for the Most Valuable Player in the NBA in 1990, it was

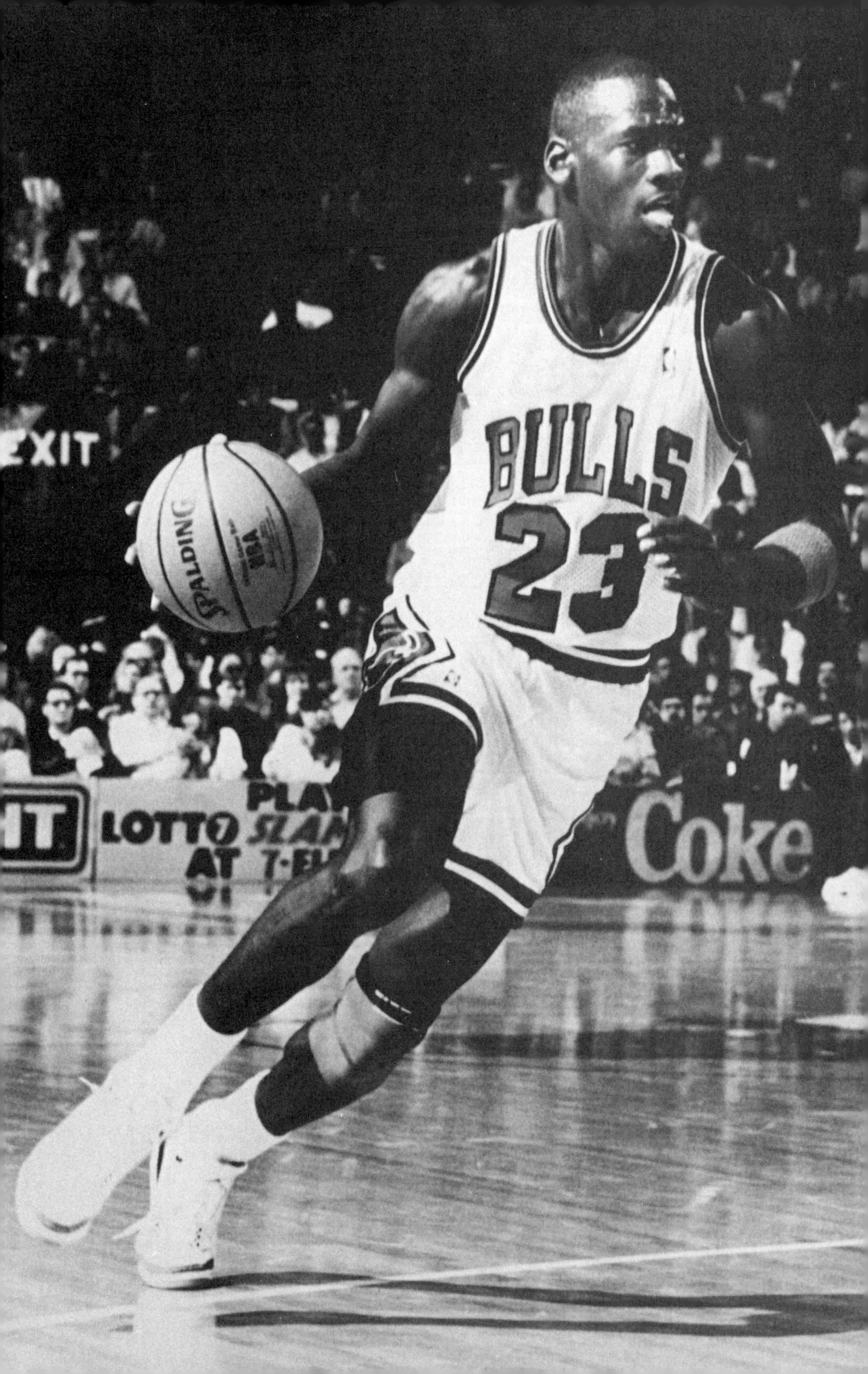
EXIT
SPALDING
BULLS
23
LOTTO 7
AT
Coke

pretty much a choice between the Chicago Bulls' Michael Jordan and the Los Angeles Lakers' Magic Johnson. Fred Kerber of the New York *Daily News* claimed it was difficult *not* to vote for Johnson, who had excelled in practically every facet of the game.

But Kerber's vote went to Jordan. His reasoning: "Take Magic from the Lakers and they'd still probably win 38 to 40 games. Take Jordan from the Bulls and they might have trouble finding the bus!"

It was true. During the late 1980s, Michael Jordan's biggest problem was finding teammates good enough to play with him.

On offense, Jordan is a scoring machine. He led the league in scoring for four straight seasons beginning in 1985–86. He is the best scoring guard in NBA history.

Many teams use at least two defensive players to try to prevent his surges to the basket. On those occasions when he doesn't score, he often ends up with a dazzling assist.

Jordan can shoot with accuracy from midrange or long distance—"downtown," as the 3-point range is sometimes called. His head bobbing and his tongue wagging, he beats defenders with either hand at different speeds from any spot on the floor.

Michael Jordan

He is also the most disruptive part of his team's defense, always among the league leaders in steals. By 1990, some observers were saying that Michael Jordan was the greatest player in the game.

Michael Jordan was born in Wilmington, North Carolina, on February 17, 1962, and brought up there. As a jug-eared tenth-grader, he couldn't make the varsity team at Laney High in Wilmington.

But stardom came fast. As a freshman at the University of North Carolina, Michael made the shot that won the NCAA title for the Tar Heels. He captured College Player of the Year trophies as a sophomore and junior and, in 1984, an Olympic gold medal. Then he signed with the Bulls.

Jordan was the NBA's Rookie of the Year in 1984–85. Sidelined with an injury through much of the following season, he returned to register 63 points in a playoff game against the Boston Celtics.

In 1986–87, the 6-foot-6 Jordan, with an average of 37.6 points per game, led the league in scoring. No player less than 7-feet tall has ever done that.

Jordan was the NBA's most valuable player in 1987–88 and again in 1990–91, the season the Bulls won their first championship. Jordan was the dominant player in the playoffs, winning MVP honors.

During his career, Jordan played on championship teams in college (1982), the Olympics (1984), and the pros (1991). Only six players in history could make that claim.

Magic Johnson

During the decade of the 1980s, the Los Angeles Lakers were often less than a perfect team. Guard Byron Scott had his share of ups and downs. Power forward A. C. Green was merely average as a shooter and rebounder. There were few better forwards than James Worthy, but he needed someone to get him the ball. Kareem Abdul-Jabbar turned 40 in 1987.

Yet the Lakers captured the division title ten straight times and the NBA championship three times during the decade.

The chief reason for the team's success: Earvin "Magic" Johnson.

Magic, a point guard, could always find a way to beat the opposition. He couldn't be picked up at full court because, at 6-foot-9, he could throw over the top. He couldn't be double-teamed because he had seemingly superhuman vision, and would zip the ball to the open man. And if the defense dropped off and dared him to shoot from 3-point range, he would—and make it.

It was Magic who, along with Larry Bird, helped to make passing popular again. During the 1970s, basketball was often a game played by what *Sports*

Illustrated called "hoop pigs." When they got their hands on the ball, they shot it. Assists were as rare as canvas sneakers. But Magic's full-court bounce pass, no-look pass, and other passing marvels were appreciated far and wide. "Passes from God," one teammate called them. Kids everywhere started imitating Magic.

Magic Johnson was born in Lansing, Michigan, on August 14, 1959, and was raised there. His father worked on an assembly line in an automobile plant. There was plenty to eat, but few luxuries. Because his father couldn't afford to buy him a bike, Magic had to do a lot of walking. He got in the habit of taking a basketball with him wherever he went, dribbling it as he walked.

After stardom at Everett High School in Lansing, Magic went on to Michigan State University. He led the Spartans to the NCAA title in 1978, helping his team defeat Larry Bird and Indiana State University in the finals.

His first pro championship is one Magic cherishes. In the sixth and deciding game of the 1980 playoffs, Magic, a rookie, got 42 points, 15 rebounds, and 7 assists as the Lakers blazed to a 123–107 win over the Philadelphia 76ers. So that he won't forget, Magic keeps a tape of the game near his VCR.

Three times the NBA's most valuable player, Magic has brought to the business world the same will to

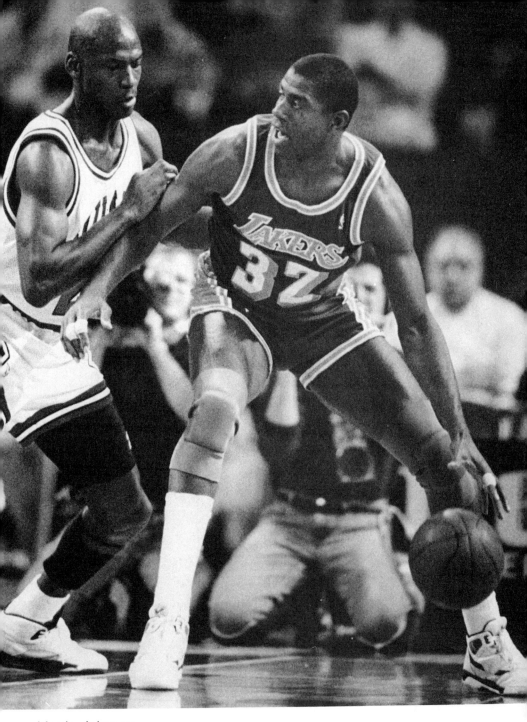

Magic Johnson

win he displays on the court. He has his own T-shirt company and his own line of clothes; there is a Nintendo game named after him. He has a very lucrative sneaker deal with Converse.

But what Magic would really like to have is his own NBA franchise. And if that's what Magic wants, don't bet he won't get it.

Kareem Abdul-Jabbar

Hank Aaron topped Babe Ruth's lifetime total of 714 home runs on April 8, 1974. Ten years minus three days later Kareem Abdul-Jabbar, with a long sweeping motion of his right arm, sent a ball soaring toward the basket at Las Vegas' Thomas and Mack Center, then the home of the Utah Jazz. The shot gave Abdul-Jabbar 31,421 career points, two more than Wilt Chamberlain's total of 31,419, till then the all-time NBA record.

Abdul-Jabbar's pursuit of that record officially began on October 18, 1969, when he scored 29 points for the Milwaukee Bucks in his first NBA game. The 7-foot-2 Kareem used his height advantage, his quickness, and his grace, to lead the league in scoring in 1970–71 and 1971–72.

Year in year out thereafter, he ranked among the league leaders in field-goal percentage and rebounding. He is the only player ever to be named the NBA's Most Valuable Player six times.

Abdul-Jabbar was born Ferdinand Lewis Alcindor, Jr., in New York City in 1947. At Power Memorial High School, he was a good student and a great basketball player. He was sought after by many colleges with big-time basketball programs. Lew chose UCLA. He went on to lead the Bruins to 88 victories in 90 games and three NCAA championships.

In his junior year at UCLA, he took the name Kareem Abdul-Jabbar when he adopted the Muslim religion. His name was legally changed in 1971.

When Kareem was in college, NCAA officials passed a rule outlawing the dunk shot. This was intended to make scoring more difficult for Kareem and giants like him. But the rule didn't stop him from averaging 26 points per game. He also made 62.4 percent of his shots, a NCAA record.

After graduating from UCLA, Kareem joined the Milwaukee Bucks of the NBA. He was traded to the Los Angeles Lakers in 1984. He was a member of six NBA championship teams.

Kareem was not always his team's most popular player. "For a long time, Kareem shut the door emotionally to a lot of people," Pat Riley, coach of the Lakers, once said. But in the final seasons of his career, the fans developed a warm feeling toward Kar-

Kareem Abdul-Jabbar

eem. Crowds that had once booed him greeted him with loud cheers and applause.

The final game of the NBA championship series in 1988–89, won by the Detroit Pistons, was the last game for Kareem after 20 seasons. He retired with over 23 NBA records to his credit, including most blocked shots (3,189), most minutes played (57,446), most field goals (15,832), and most points (38,387).

"Kareem scored 15,000 of his points with sky-hooks, dunks, and finger rolls," Kansas City coach Cotton Fitzsimmons once said of him. "The other 16,000 he got by using his head. He's predictable, but that doesn't mean you can stop him. You can't."

Larry Bird

Forward Larry Bird, the Celtics' star throughout the 1980s, and the only noncenter to win the NBA's Most Valuable Player award three times, was never very fast or agile. Nor could he jump. And the one-hand push shot he favored was from another era.

What Bird did do was excel in every phase of the game—shooting, passing, rebounding, and defense.

Take passing. Bird was incredible. He would dribble down one side of the court, stop, go up for his shot, spot an open teammate at the top of his jump, and fire the ball to him. Or he'd knife through the middle, take a pass, and then, without looking, flip the ball over his shoulder to a teammate cutting underneath.

And Bird was always aware of what was going on around him. "I guess the key thing is that I always know what is happening on the court," he once said. "I know exactly what I can and cannot do. I know when and how I can score on a particular defender."

Larry Bird was born in French Lick, a small town in southern Indiana. "A hick from French Lick," is how he once described himself. He was the fourth boy in a family of five boys and a girl.

At Spring Valley High in French Lick, Larry made up his mind to become a star on the basketball team. He didn't own a car or have much spending money, so he and his friends practiced basketball. They practiced until school closed and then found a playground where they could practice until dark.

Bird set a conference scoring record as a high school senior and received seven trophies at his school's awards banquet. He got so many college scholarship offers, he had trouble making up his mind what school to choose. He picked Indiana University. But it was too big and he felt out of place. He ended up at Indiana State University, a much smaller school.

After an exceptional college career, Bird joined the Boston Celtics. He was the team leader in scoring, rebounding, and minutes played in 1979–80. The

Larry Bird

same year, he won the NBA's Rookie of the Year honors.

He continued to work hard on his game. Three hours before any game at the Boston Garden, Bird could be found out on the floor. He always followed the same routine: first, medium-range shots from the sides, then shots from the free-throw line, followed by 3-pointers. Sometimes he'd take one hundred shots; sometimes it was two hundred or three hundred.

Bird helped the Celtics win the NBA championship in 1980–81, 1983–84, and 1985–86. He was the league's MVP in 1983–84, 1984–85, and 1985–86.

Beginning in 1986–87 and continuing for the next three seasons, the Celtics had good teams but were eliminated in the early rounds of the playoffs. Bird missed 76 regular-season games because of surgery in 1988–89. The following season, he lacked his long-range shooting touch and was erratic on defense. For the first time in his career, he heard criticism from his teammates.

During the off-season, Bird always went back to Indiana. He spent his time mowing his mother's lawn, shooting baskets on his own regulation basketball court, and hanging out with friends.

French Lick will always be his home. It's where he feels he belongs. Said a reporter who covered the Celtics: "When his career is over, he'll be out of Boston so fast, all you'll see is his exhaust."

Julius Erving

Julius Erving, the most exciting player of his time, or perhaps of *any* time, was once asked what it was that enabled him to perform his incredible dunks and other spectacular moves.

"It's easy," Erving answered, "once you learn how to fly."

As a star performer for the Philadelphia 76ers during the 1980s, Erving, or Dr. J, as he was known, played the game with imagination, with a creative spirit. To Julius, basketball was an art form, like music or painting.

"My overall goal," he once told *Esquire* magazine, "is to give people the feeling they are being entertained by an artist—and to win."

Julius Erving was born in East Meadow, New York, in 1950 and was brought up in nearby Roosevelt. Both are Long Island communities within about forty-five minutes' commuting distance of New York City.

Julius learned basketball on the asphalt courts of Roosevelt Park, not far from his home. One day when he was in sixth grade, and not yet 6 feet tall, he leaped high and in the air slammed the ball down through the hoop—his first dunk. As a seventh-grader, he was able to palm the ball.

At Roosevelt High, Julius concentrated on playing team basketball instead of trying to gain the spotlight with flashy moves. He was named to the All Long Island High School Team as a senior and received more than one hundred scholarship offers from colleges. He chose the University of Massachusetts.

Julius set records for scoring and rebounding, and, as a sophomore and again as a junior, helped to earn his team a bid to the National Invitation Tournament. After his junior year, Julius left college to join the

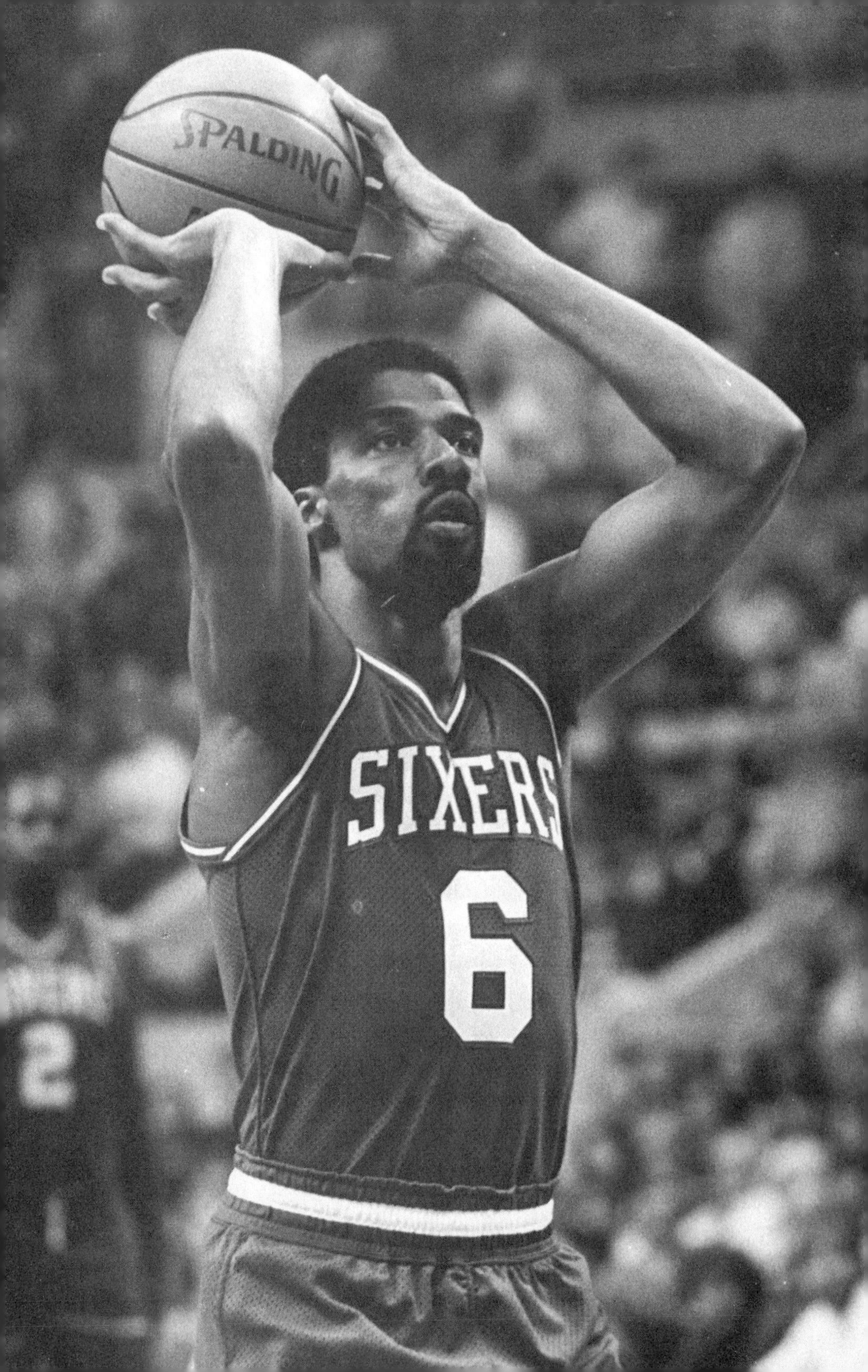
SPALDING
SIXERS
6

Virginia Squires of the American Basketball Association, a professional league that had begun operation in 1967.

Erving quickly made a name for himself as a basketball acrobat with his leaping, whirling, and spinning moves. His specialty was a soaring dunk from the foul line. Sometimes he jammed the ball in with his "tomahawk" slam. Other times, he stuffed it in with his back to the basket. Even opposing players would shake their heads in disbelief.

Although Erving was the ABA's greatest star, the Squires lost money. When the club sought to trade Julius, he ended up with the New York Nets. In 1976, the ABA folded and four of its teams were taken into the NBA. Julius was traded to the 76ers.

The Sixers reached the NBA's championship finals in 1980 and 1982. But not until 1983, with Julius contributing countless slams, steals, and blocked shots, did the team win the title.

The season of 1986–87 was Erving's last. In city after city throughout the league, huge crowds turned out to see him. From the time he stripped off his warm-up suit, the fans in each city cheered his every move. They had come to see him a final time, to be thrilled by one more soaring, heart-stopping dunk.

Julius Erving

No player, not Kareem Abdul-Jabbar, not Bill Russell or Wilt Chamberlain, received that kind of tribute.

Bill Russell

Bill Russell, star center of the Boston Celtics throughout the 1960s, was in a class by himself as a defensive player. It's generally agreed that the 6-foot-10 Russell was the best rebounder and shot blocker ever to have played the game. He could outjump any of his opponents. This ability, plus his great pride and determination, produced what was almost an unbeatable combination.

The evidence is clear. In his thirteen seasons as a member of the Celtics, he led the team to the NBA championship eleven times.

"Led" is the appropriate word. Russell not only contributed defensively, he was always an unselfish player, just as eager to feed a teammate as put the ball up himself.

Born in Monroe, Louisiana, in 1934, Russell was raised in Oakland, California. He was not a standout high school player but showed enough talent to be offered a scholarship to the University of San Francisco. "It was the only scholarship offer I got," Russell

Bill Russell

said later, "so I took it." He helped steer his team to the NCAA title in 1955 and 1956.

The year Russell graduated from college, 1956, was an Olympic year. Before becoming a professional, he played for the United States Olympic basketball team, helping the team win a gold medal.

As a professional, Russell continued his winning habits. "Nobody ever blocked shots in the pros before Russell came along," Red Auerbach, the Celtics' coach, said of him. "He upsets everybody. The only defense they can think to dish out is a physical beating."

Russell's defensive skills, the playmaking of Bob Cousy, and Bill Sharman's deadly jumpers were key factors as Boston captured the NBA championship in 1956–57. It was the team's first title in what was to become one of the great dynasties in professional sports.

Three years after Russell made his debut with the Celtics, Wilt Chamberlain, who was to become the game's most devastating scorer, came into the league. Their first meeting—on November 7, 1959—was a historic struggle. The more experienced Russell out-dueled the rookie Chamberlain that night. He also managed to outplay the younger man in most of their encounters over the years that followed.

Chamberlain carved out a brilliant career, displaying an ability to score as no pro player before him had and very few since have. But the championships always seemed to go to the Celtics. "I'd rather be what I am, with a champion," Russell once said, "than the best scorer in the league with a team that never wins."

After his retirement, Russell served as a TV analyst for NBA games. He was back in basketball as a coach of the Seattle Supersonics in 1973, a job he held for four years. He tried coaching again with the Sacramento Kings in 1987.

One criticism of coach Russell was that he was too impatient with young players. He looked for greatness from them. Maybe all he wanted them to do was play as Bill Russell had played. That, perhaps, was too much to ask.

Wilt Chamberlain

No one has ever hit five home runs in a baseball game or scored six touchdowns in a football game. Should either of these ever be achieved, it would be compared to what twenty-six-year-old Wilt Chamberlain did on the night of March 2, 1962.

Wilt's team, the Philadelphia Warriors, had traveled to Hershey, Pennsylvania, to play the New York Knicks on a neutral court. The Warriors had clinched

second place in the NBA's Eastern Division and were waiting for the playoffs to begin. The Knicks were in last place, winding up a dismal season.

As the game got underway, Chamberlain began scoring at a frantic pace. He had an amazing 23 points at the end of the first quarter, 41 points at the end of the first half.

When the game resumed, Chamberlain kept pouring in points. He had 69 points at the end of the third quarter. Once the fourth quarter began, Wilt's teammates attempted to get the ball to him whenever possible.

Wilt's total hit 80, then 90. With about one minute remaining in the game, Chamberlain reached up near the basket to grab a pass. With a graceful sweeping motion, he slammed the ball through. It was his 100th point, the all-time record for a game.

In the years since, no one has come close to scoring 100 points in a game. The next-highest total is 78, also scored by Wilt.

An awesome, powerful figure, the 7-foot-1 Chamberlain is remembered for his scoring ability. He led the NBA in points scored for seven straight seasons beginning in 1958–59. His career-total 31,410 points

Wilt Chamberlain

is second only to Kareem Abdul-Jabbar's total of 38,387.

A Philadelphia native, Chamberlain was one of the most publicized high school basketball players in history. He went from Philadelphia's Overbrook High School to the University of Kansas. After two years of college ball, he dropped out. He joined the Philadelphia Warriors of the NBA the following year.

As a member of the NBA, Chamberlain had two stays in Philadelphia, one with the Warriors, the other with the 76ers. He ended his career with the Los Angeles Lakers, a team he steered to the NBA championship in 1971. He was named the NBA's Most Valuable Player four times.

Chamberlain's best season as a scorer was 1961–62. He finished with 4,029 points in 80 games, an average of 50.4 points per game. That's another record that still stands.

But Chamberlain could do much more than put the ball in the basket. During 1967–68, he led the NBA in assists and rebounds. And he ended his career with more rebounds per game than Bill Russell—22.8 vs. 22.4, even though Russell is the standard by which all rebounders are judged.

However, Chamberlain never won any praise as a foul shooter. His average was usually below .600. High school players do better than that.

Yet he can be forgiven whatever failings he had. He was the dominant figure in almost every game he played. "He gets the points, he gets the ball, and he can go all night," is how Bob Cousy once described him. "What else can you say?"

George Mikan

Before Kareem Abdul-Jabbar, before Wilt Chamberlain and Bill Russell, there was George Mikan, the first great center. The 6-foot-10, 245-pound Mikan, who starred for the Minneapolis Lakers (they moved to Los Angeles in 1960) from 1947 to 1956, led his team to five NBA championships and topped the league in scoring five times. Once, in a game against the Rochester Royals, Mikan scored 62 points, his all-time high.

George Mikan was born in Joliet, Illinois, in 1924. In high school, he towered above his classmates. As center on the basketball team, he had a height advantage over his opponents, but he was clumsy and slow-footed. When he sought a scholarship to Notre Dame, the coach turned him down. "He's too awkward," the coach told an assistant. "Besides, he wears glasses."

George was later offered a scholarship by Chicago's DePaul University. The coach there made him skip

rope to improve his agility. He also made him practice hook shots by the hour. The shot was to become
his trademark.

The hard work paid dividends. Mikan won All-
America honors in 1944, 1945, and 1946.

As a pro player, he quickly became the game's top
scorer. The Lakers' attack was as subtle as a call for
help. Once Minneapolis got possession, George
would lumber into the pivot spot and wait for the ball
to be passed to him. He'd then drop in a hook shot
or, using his height and strength, power his way to
the basket. "Trying to stop Mikan was like stepping
into the path of a bulldozer," John Devaney, onetime
editor of *Sport* magazine, said of him.

His opponents weren't the only ones to try to stop
No. 99. So did the rule makers, who widened the foul
lane from 6 to 12 feet. (It was changed to its present
16 feet in 1956.) Since an offensive player was not
permitted to remain in the lane for more than three
seconds, Mikan was forced to shoot more from the
outside. The "Mikan rule," as it was called, caused
George's scoring average to drop by several points.

In 1950, Mikan was chosen as the greatest basketball player of the first fifty years of the twentieth cen-

George Mikan

tury. He retired from the game in 1955 to become a lawyer.

Hank Luisetti

Babe Ruth changed baseball for all time with his home runs. Football was revolutionized during the 1930s and 1940s by the great passing of Sammy Baugh of the Washington Redskins.

During these years, basketball also had a player who triggered sweeping changes in the game. His name was Angelo "Hank" Luisetti. He was the first player to shoot the running one-hand jumper, foreshadowing the arrival of Magic Johnson, Michael Jordan, and other such wizards of the present day.

A skinny forward for Galileo High School in San Francisco in the early 1930s, Luisetti was not an outstanding scorer. He was known for his ball-handling abilities, his clever dribbling and pinpoint passes. He did so many things so well that he won a scholarship to Stanford University.

In a game at Stanford in 1935, the 6-foot, 2-inch Luisetti began popping one-handers on the run. "It was bang, bang, bang," Stanford coach John Bunn once recalled. Luisetti scored 35 points. "The one-

Hank Luisetti

hander looks weird," Bunn told Luisetti. "But stick with it."

The reason the one-hander looked weird was that no one used it. Coaches in those days taught that there were only two right ways to shoot. You could drive in for a lay-up or stop, plant your feet, and take a two-handed set shot.

On December 30, 1936, Luisetti, then a sophomore, led the Stanford team into New York City for a game at Madison Square Garden against Long Island University. By playing an old-style, ball-control offense, and shooting in the traditional manner, LIU had won 43 straight games. No one gave Stanford a chance.

But the West Coast team shocked the experts by routing LIU, 45–31. Luisetti alone scored 15 points with his deft one-handers. That's not a big number by today's standards, but in 1935 it was enough to stun the basketball world. Within weeks, kids in playgrounds and gyms all over the country were flipping the ball up one-handed.

In his three years at Stanford, Luisetti scored 1,596 points, setting an all-time college record. In 1938, he scored 50 points against Duquesne, becoming the first college player to get that many points in a game.

Luisetti served in the Navy during World War II. Not long before he was discharged, he got spinal meningitis, a serious illness. This, plus other physical problems, dashed any hopes he might have had for a pro career.

When sportswriters voted for the greatest basketball player of the first half of the century in 1956, Luisetti ranked second only to the great George Mikan. In 1959, he was one of the first players elected to the Basketball Hall of Fame.

BASKETBALL WORDS AND TERMS

American Basketball Association (ABA)—A professional league that operated from 1967–68 through 1975–76.

American Basketball League (ABL)—A professional league that was founded in 1926 and that operated until the late 1930s. A second ABL began operation in 1961, but folded the following season.

Assist—A pass by an offensive player that leads directly to a basket.

Backboard—The flat surface to which the basket is attached.

Backcourt—The defensive team's half of the court.

Basket—The metal ring, 18 inches in diameter, with a net of cord, 15 to 18 inches in length, through which the ball must pass for a score to be recorded.

Basketball Association of America (BAA)—A professional league that was founded in 1946. It was re-
named the National Basketball Association in
1949.

Boards—The backboard. Also, rebounds.

Box Out—Action of a defensive player who blocks an
opponent's path to a rebound by standing between the player and the basket.

Center—The player who normally plays the pivot
and takes part in the center jump. The center is
often called the pivotman.

Division Line—The line that divides the court in two;
the center line; also called halfcourt line.

Double Dribble—Dribbling the ball with both hands
at the same time, or dribbling, stopping, and
then starting again. Double dribble is a violation.

Double-team—To use two defenders to guard an offensive player.

Dribble—To move the ball by means of repeated
bounces.

Dunk—A field goal made by slamming the ball
through the basket from above the rim.

End Line—The line at each end of the court that runs
the width of the court and joins the two sidelines.

Fast Break—The quick movement of the ball downcourt by a team that has gained possession
through a defensive rebound.

Forecourt—The half of the court containing the offensive team's basket.

Forward—One of two players who, with the center, normally makes up the front line of a team's offense. At the tipoff, the forwards line up nearest the opposition team's basket.

Foul—Any infraction of the rules.

Free Throw—An unhindered shot at the basket from behind the free-throw line that is awarded to a player when an opposing player has committed a personal or technical foul. A successful free throw is worth one point.

Free-throw Lane—The area at each end of the court defined by a pair of parallel lines 12 feet apart (16 feet apart in the NBA), the foul line, and the end line. No player may remain within the free-throw lane for more than three seconds (unless he or she is contesting a rebound).

Freeze—To retain possession of the ball without any attempt to score (to prevent the opposition from gaining possession and scoring).

Frontcourt—The offensive team's half of the court.

Give-and-go—An offensive tactic in which one player passes to a teammate and then gets into position for a return pass.

Goaltending—To illegally interfere with the flight of a field-goal attempt when the ball is above the rim of the basket. If goaltending is called on the defense, the shot is scored as a field goal. When goaltending is called on the offensive team, the defensive team is awarded possession of the ball and no points are scored.

Guard—One of two players who are responsible for bringing the ball into the frontcourt and starting offensive plays. Guards normally play farthest from the basket.

Held Ball—A situation in which a player for each team is in possession of the ball at the same time. In the NBA, possession is determined by a jump ball between the two players. In high school and college play, one team is awarded possession after a held ball is called; the other team gets possession after the next held ball.

Jump Ball—A method of putting the ball in play in which the referee tosses the ball up between two opposing players; each player jumps and attempts to tap the ball to a teammate. A jump ball is the method of putting the ball in play at the beginning of a period or, in the NBA, when a held ball is called.

Keyhole, Key—A court area that includes the free-throw lane, the foul line, and the foul circle.

Lay-up—A usually one-handed, banked shot that is made close to the basket.

Loose-ball Foul—A foul committed by a player in pursuit of a free ball or rebound.

National Association of Intercollegiate Athletics (NAIA)—An organization that administers intercollegiate basketball among schools with small enrollments.

National Basketball Association (NBA)—A professional league consisting of 27 teams (as of 1990–91), founded in 1946 as the Basketball Association of America. The NBA adopted its present name in 1949.

National Collegiate Athletic Association (NCAA)—An organization that administers men's and women's college basketball, enforcing rules, publishing statistics, and conducting championship tournaments.

National Invitation Tournament (NIT)—A postseason tournament founded in 1937–38 and now sponsored by the New York Metropolitan Intercollegiate Basketball Association.

Outlet Pass—A long pass that triggers a fast break.

Personal Foul—Charging, hacking, blocking, pushing, elbowing, or other such foul that involves physical contact with an opponent. A player fouled in the act of shooting is given one free throw if the field goal is successful, two free throws if it is not.

Pick—A screen set by a player that enables a teammate to move to the basket with the ball or cut to an open area of the court for a pass.

Pivot—*See* Post.

Pivotman—The center or forward who plays the post.

Post (or Pivot)—A position either near the foul line or under the basket taken by the center or a forward, who stands with his back to the basket and serves as the hub of the offense, relaying passes, providing screens, and shooting.

Post Up—To play the post position; to act as pivotman.

Press—Tight guarding by the defensive team.

Rebound—A missed shot that bounces off the backboard or rim.

Referee—One of two officials responsible for conducting a game. In professional play, both officials are called referees. The referee with the longer term of service is in charge. In high school and college play, one official is called the umpire. In practice, however, both are referees.

Sag—A defensive tactic in which one or more players drop off the player they are guarding to cover the center or a forward near the basket.

Screen—A move by an offensive player to position his body so it acts as a barrier from behind which a teammate with the ball can shoot.

Sixth Man—The first substitute to come off the bench. Or, a team's most valuable substitute player.

Steal—A play in which a defensive player legally takes the ball from an opponent.

Switch—To change from guarding one's own man to guarding a teammate's.

Team Foul—A foul charged to a team when a personal foul is committed by one of its players. When a team exceeds its quota of team fouls, the opposition is awarded a bonus free throw on all subsequent fouls.

Technical Foul—An infraction of the rules that does not ordinarily involve contact between players. It can be called against a player, a nonplayer on the bench, or a coach for such infractions as delaying the game or unsportsmanlike conduct. One free throw is awarded to the other team.

Ten-second Rule—A rule stating that the offensive team must advance the ball across the division line within ten seconds or lose possession.

Three-second Rule—A rule that states an offensive player cannot remain within the free-throw lane or circle for more than three seconds.

Tip-in—A field goal made by flicking a rebound into the basket.

Tip-off (or Tap-off)—The jump ball that starts a period of play.

Trap—To double-team an opponent with the ball.

Traveling—A violation that occurs when a player takes more steps than are allowed while holding the ball or dribbling.

Turnover—A play in which the offensive team loses possession of the ball without taking a shot.

Umpire—In high school and college basketball, one of two officials responsible for the conduct of a game.

Violation—Traveling, double dribbling, or other such infraction of the rules, not including personal or technical fouls. A violation is penalized by loss of possession.

ALL-TIME NBA RECORDS

Most Seasons—20, Kareem Abdul-Jabbar

Most Games, Career—1,560, Kareem Abdul-Jabbar

Most Points, Lifetime—38,387, Kareem Abdul-Jabbar

Most Points, Season—4,029, Wilt Chamberlain, Philadelphia, 1961–62

Most Points, Game—100, Wilt Chamberlain, Philadelphia vs. New York at Hershey, Pennsylvania, March 2, 1962

Most Field Goals, Career—15,837, Kareem Abdul-Jabbar

Most Field Goals, Season—1,597, Wilt Chamberlain, Philadelphia, 1961–62

Most Field Goals, Game—36, Wilt Chamberlain, Philadelphia vs. New York at Hershey, Pennsylvania, March 2, 1962

Most Three-Point Field Goals, Career—568, Dale Ellis

Most Three-Point Field Goals, Season—166, Michael Adams, Denver, 1988–89

Most Three-Point Field Goals, Game—9, Dale Ellis, Seattle vs. Los Angeles Clippers, April 20, 1990

Highest Free-Throw Percentage, Career—.900, Rick Barry (3,818/4,243)

Most Free Throws Made, Career—7,694, Oscar Robertson

Most Free Throws Made, Season—840, Jerry West, Los Angeles Lakers, 1965–66

Most Free Throws Made, Game—28, Wilt Chamberlain, Philadelphia vs. New York, Hershey, Pennsylvania, March 2, 1962

Most Rebounds, Career—23,924, Wilt Chamberlain

Most Rebounds, Season—2,149, Wilt Chamberlain, Philadelphia, 1960–61

Most Rebounds, Game—55, Wilt Chamberlain, Philadelphia vs. Boston, November 24, 1960

Most Assists, Career—9,887, Oscar Robertson

Most Assists, Season—1,128, John Stockton, Utah, 1987–88

Most Assists, Game—29, Kevin Porter, New Jersey vs. Houston, February 24, 1978

Most Personal Fouls, Career—4,657, Kareem Abdul-Jabbar

Most Personal Fouls, Season—386, Darryl Dawkins, New Jersey, 1983–84

Most Personal Fouls, Game—8, Don Otten, Tri Cities at Sheboygan, November 24, 1949

Highest Team Winning Percentage, Season—.841, Los Angeles Lakers, 1971–72 (69–13)

Lowest Team Winning Percentage, Season—.110, Philadelphia Warriors, 1972–73 (9–73)

Most Consecutive Games Won—33, Los Angeles Lakers, November 5, 1971–January 7, 1972

Most Points, Game, One Team—186, Detroit at Denver, December 13, 1983 (three overtimes)

Fewest Points, Game, One Team—57, Milwaukee vs. Boston, at Providence, February 27, 1955

Most Points, Game, Both Teams—370, Detroit (186) at Denver (184), December 13, 1983 (three overtimes)

Fewest Points, Game, Both Teams—119, Milwaukee (57) vs. Boston (62) at Providence, February 27, 1955

INDEX

Page numbers in italics indicate a photograph or diagram.